BOSTON

A HISTORY & CELEBRATION

NEIL WRIGHT

PRODUCED IN COLLABORATION WITH THE HISTORY OF BOSTON PROJECT

THE FRANCIS FRITH COLLECTION

www.francisfrith.co.uk

First published in the United Kingdom in 2005
by The Francis Frith Collection®

Hardback Edition 2005
ISBN 1-84589-196-1

Text and Design copyright © The Francis Frith Collection®
Photographs copyright © The Francis Frith Collection®
except where indicated

The Frith® photographs and the Frith® logo are reproduced under licence
from Heritage Photographic Resources Ltd, the owners of the Frith® archive
and trademarks
'The Francis Frith Collection', 'Francis Frith' and 'Frith' are registered trademarks
of Heritage Photographic Resources Ltd.

British Library Cataloguing in Publication Data

Boston - A History & Celebration
Neil Wright,
Produced in collaboration with the History of Boston Project

The Francis Frith Collection
Frith's Barn, Teffont,
Salisbury, Wiltshire SP3 5QP
Tel: +44 (0) 1722 716 376
Email: info@francisfrith.co.uk
www.francisfrith.co.uk

Printed and bound in England

Front Cover: **BOSTON, DOUGHTY QUAY 1890** 26066t

Additional modern (2005) photographs by Neil Wright unless otherwise specified.

Domesday extract used in timeline by kind permission of
Alecto Historical Editions, www.domesdaybook.org
Aerial photographs reproduced under licence from
Simmons Aerofilms Limited.
Historical Ordnance Survey maps reproduced under licence from Homecheck.co.uk

Every attempt has been made to contact copyright holders of illustrative material.
We will be happy to give full acknowledgement in future editions for any items not
credited. Any information should be directed to The Francis Frith Collection.

*The colour-tinting in this book is for illustrative purposes only,
and is not intended to be historically accurate*

AS WITH ANY HISTORICAL DATABASE, THE FRANCIS FRITH ARCHIVE
IS CONSTANTLY BEING CORRECTED AND IMPROVED, AND THE
PUBLISHERS WOULD WELCOME INFORMATION ON OMISSIONS OR
INACCURACIES

CONTENTS

BOSTON FROM THE AIR 1930 AF31901

BOSTON
A HISTORY & CELEBRATION

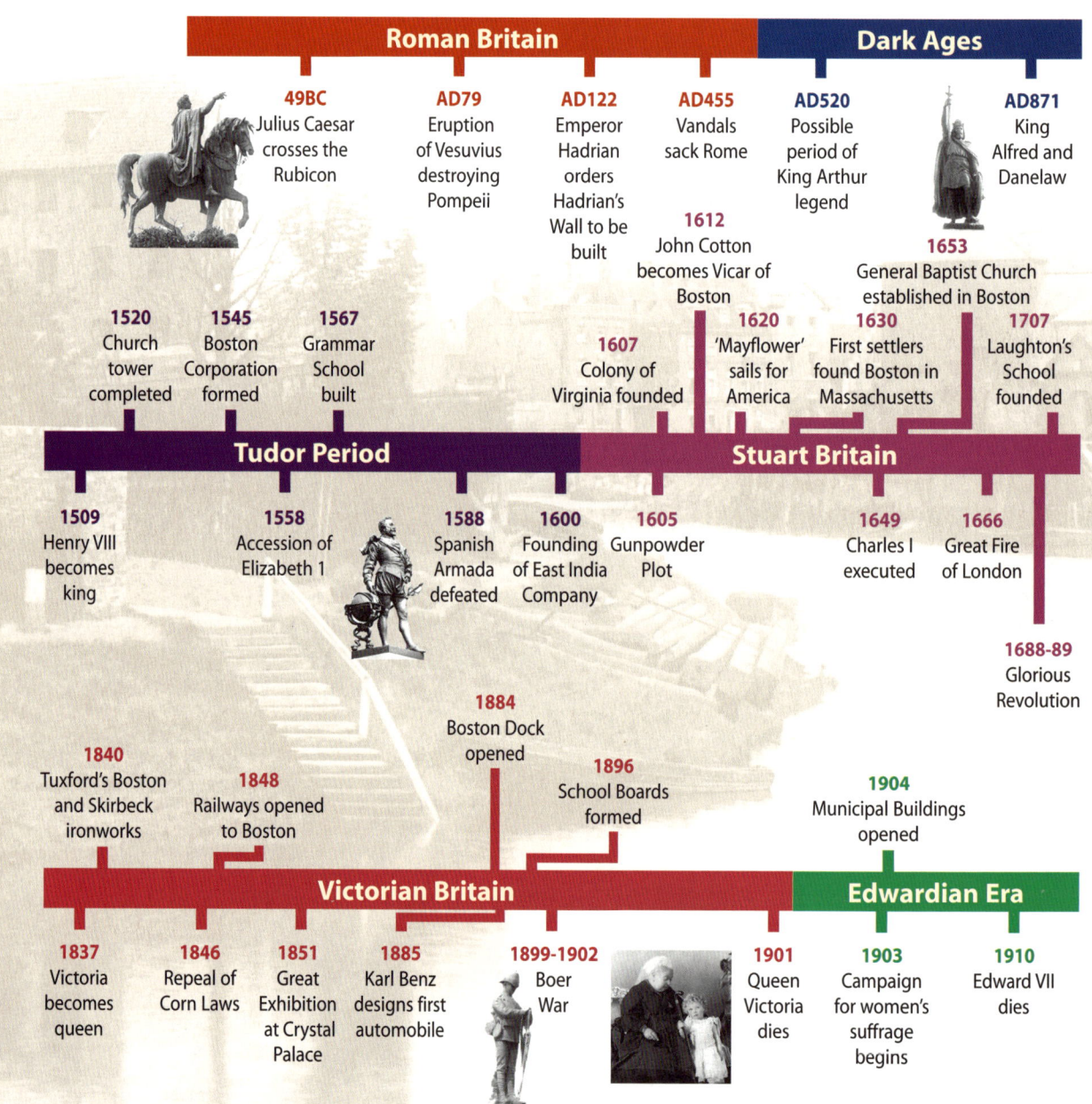

Roman Britain

49BC
Julius Caesar crosses the Rubicon

AD79
Eruption of Vesuvius destroying Pompeii

AD122
Emperor Hadrian orders Hadrian's Wall to be built

AD455
Vandals sack Rome

Dark Ages

AD520
Possible period of King Arthur legend

AD871
King Alfred and Danelaw

1612
John Cotton becomes Vicar of Boston

1653
General Baptist Church established in Boston

1520
Church tower completed

1545
Boston Corporation formed

1567
Grammar School built

1607
Colony of Virginia founded

1620
'Mayflower' sails for America

1630
First settlers found Boston in Massachusetts

1707
Laughton's School founded

Tudor Period

Stuart Britain

1509
Henry VIII becomes king

1558
Accession of Elizabeth 1

1588
Spanish Armada defeated

1600
Founding of East India Company

1605
Gunpowder Plot

1649
Charles I executed

1666
Great Fire of London

1688-89
Glorious Revolution

1884
Boston Dock opened

1840
Tuxford's Boston and Skirbeck ironworks

1848
Railways opened to Boston

1896
School Boards formed

1904
Municipal Buildings opened

Victorian Britain

Edwardian Era

1837
Victoria becomes queen

1846
Repeal of Corn Laws

1851
Great Exhibition at Crystal Palace

1885
Karl Benz designs first automobile

1899-1902
Boer War

1901
Queen Victoria dies

1903
Campaign for women's suffrage begins

1910
Edward VII dies

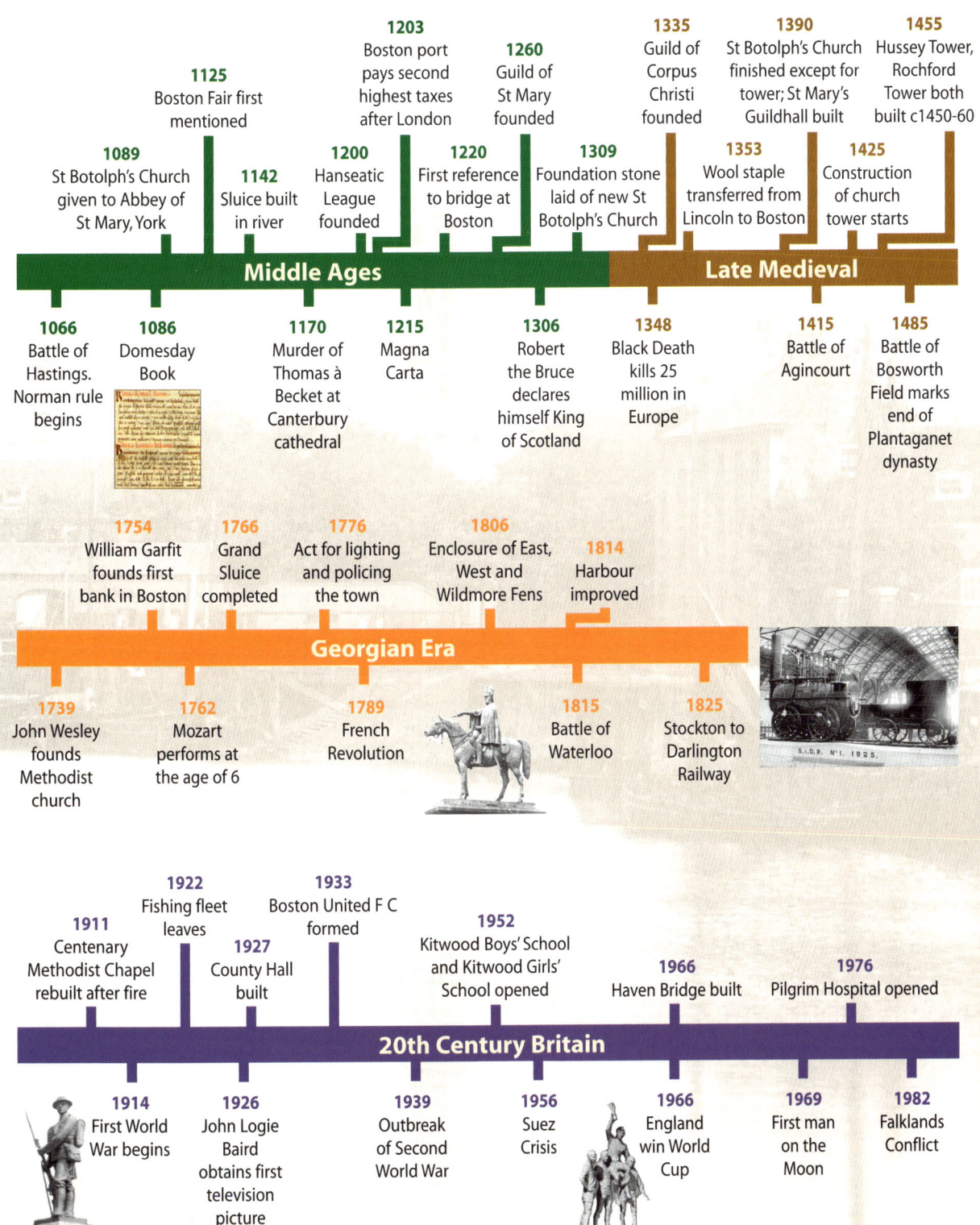

Middle Ages

1089 St Botolph's Church given to Abbey of St Mary, York

1125 Boston Fair first mentioned

1142 Sluice built in river

1200 Hanseatic League founded

1203 Boston port pays second highest taxes after London

1220 First reference to bridge at Boston

1260 Guild of St Mary founded

1309 Foundation stone laid of new St Botolph's Church

1066 Battle of Hastings. Norman rule begins

1086 Domesday Book

1170 Murder of Thomas à Becket at Canterbury cathedral

1215 Magna Carta

1306 Robert the Bruce declares himself King of Scotland

Late Medieval

1335 Guild of Corpus Christi founded

1390 St Botolph's Church finished except for tower; St Mary's Guildhall built

1455 Hussey Tower, Rochford Tower both built c1450-60

1353 Wool staple transferred from Lincoln to Boston

1425 Construction of church tower starts

1348 Black Death kills 25 million in Europe

1415 Battle of Agincourt

1485 Battle of Bosworth Field marks end of Plantaganet dynasty

Georgian Era

1754 William Garfit founds first bank in Boston

1766 Grand Sluice completed

1776 Act for lighting and policing the town

1806 Enclosure of East, West and Wildmore Fens

1814 Harbour improved

1739 John Wesley founds Methodist church

1762 Mozart performs at the age of 6

1789 French Revolution

1815 Battle of Waterloo

1825 Stockton to Darlington Railway

20th Century Britain

1911 Centenary Methodist Chapel rebuilt after fire

1922 Fishing fleet leaves

1927 County Hall built

1933 Boston United F C formed

1952 Kitwood Boys' School and Kitwood Girls' School opened

1966 Haven Bridge built

1976 Pilgrim Hospital opened

1914 First World War begins

1926 John Logie Baird obtains first television picture

1939 Outbreak of Second World War

1956 Suez Crisis

1966 England win World Cup

1969 First man on the Moon

1982 Falklands Conflict

CHAPTER ONE

MEDIEVAL BOSTON

BOSTON has existed as a town and a port for over 900 years, and the ghost of that early settlement can be seen in the plan of the present streets. Nowadays Skirbeck is a suburb of Boston, but it seems that in the early days things were the other way round. In the Domesday Book of 1086, Boston is not listed as a separate place; in fact, it was a new development on a greenfield site in the parish of Skirbeck.

So how did it start? In brief, a Norman knight, who came over with William in 1066, spotted a gap in the market and took advantage of it. The site for Boston was based on a river crossing at the mouth of the River Witham, where routes from the east, north and south-west converged. By 1066 there might have been a small village here but 1,000 years before, in Roman times, the site was a couple of low-lying offshore islands, and part of the Witham followed the channel between them. These were part of a long line of little islands between the Wash and a vast shallow lagoon that silted up over the centuries to become the fens. The islands were small and lacked fresh water so not many people would want to live on them; Roman archaeological finds show there were at least a few people working here on the production of salt. Over the centuries the shallow waters of the lagoon filled with silt brought down by the rivers, and the land rose so that the tides no longer came in regularly. The line of islands became a continuous strip, called the 'townlands', with fens north of them and Wash marshes to the south. The fens were still not a desirable place to live because they

were covered by freshwater floods for several months of the year, and after a parching summer they became a desert. The townlands near the coast were a bit more attractive than the fens as they were above the floodplain.

When the Roman army left Britain early in the 5th century, the fens had been largely abandoned; it was another 100 years before Saxon settlers founded the first villages on the townlands in a border region between competing kingdoms. A century later they were converted to Christianity, and this was Anglo-Saxon territory for another 200 years. Recent excavations have indicated that a site in Fishtoft may have been an early Anglo-Saxon monastery. But then the Viking's Great Army landed in East Anglia in 865 and conquered kingdom after kingdom. The Vikings were pagans and, as churches were looted and burnt, the surviving Christians fled to the safety of Saxon territory to the west. It is believed that Viking warriors started to put down roots in Lincolnshire after 877 and, from then on, the Danes lived alongside Saxon neighbours in the county. The English re-conquered Lincolnshire between 918 and 942 but the Anglo-Danish aristocracy continued to rule the county under the West Saxon king, and people in Lincolnshire continued to speak Scandinavian for centuries.

Skirbeck is the Danish name for an area that includes the site where Boston was later built and, by 1066, Skirbeck and other villages had been settled on this curving strip of land, sometimes only a mile wide, that extended for many miles around the Wash. The townland villages continued to reclaim land on both sides - from the inland fen and the saltwater marshes - and had to build banks, sluices, drains and bridges to keep their land. It was to be another 700 years before any villages were settled in the fens themselves. The wild and remote environment, and the absence of great landed estates, stimulated the sense of personal freedom and self-reliance that has been so strong in the past, and is still strong today. But people soon realised how interdependent all the townland villages were; only by working for the common good, and not relying on external powers, were they able to carve out a prosperous life from the wilderness.

As you drive around the Boston area, you can tell whether you are on the townlands or the fens because the roads on the townlands have many twists and bends, reminding us of the old verse that 'the rolling English drunkard made the rolling English road'. On the other hand, the roads on the fens were only created some 200 years ago, and are long and straight with right-angled junctions.

We can now go back to that Norman knight who had spotted a gap in the market. His name was Alan the Red, and he was well-connected by being the son of the Count of Ponthievre and a relative of the Duke of Brittany. King William gave him a number of manors that had previously belonged to Edwin, the last Saxon Earl of Mercia, and these included land that became the eastern half of Boston. This manor was later called Hallgarth and Alan's whole collection of manors became the Honour of Richmond, so-called because its headquarters were at Richmond Castle in north Yorkshire. Alan's successors as lords

of the manor became Dukes of Brittany in the 13th century so, periodically, when there was strife between England and France, the Earldom of Richmond was seized by the Crown and passed to other great nobles or members of the royal family. The townlands were notable for having many small manors and, at Boston, the land west of the River Witham was divided between two other manors, and developed as a separate suburb.

ST BOTOLPH

Boston takes its name from the parish church which is dedicated to the Saxon monk St Botolph. The town was called 'St Botolph's' or 'Botolph's Town' until about 1400, but since then the shorter name 'Boston' has always been used. St Botolph was given land by the King of the South Angles in 654 to found a monastery at a place called Ikanho. The saint died in Suffolk, which is in the territory of the South Angles, and parts of his body were carried to the monasteries at Ely, Thorney and Bury St Edmunds, so it is likely that Ikanho was near the village of Iken in Suffolk.

The opportunity that Alan had spotted was that his property near the mouth of the Witham was ideally placed to handle the trade of the city of Lincoln, 30 miles upstream, which was then one of the most important and wealthiest cities in England. The 11th and 12th centuries were a time of peace in Europe, at least compared with the

Behind the buildings on the right was the Mart Yard with the Manor House at the far end.

A VIEW FROM THE FERRY 1893 32063

Viking period before then, so international trade flourished, particularly in fine goods like cloth and wine, and reached levels not known since the withdrawal of Rome from these shores. When the Fossdyke Canal from Lincoln to the Trent was re-opened people from Yorkshire and the Midlands could also do their trading through Boston.

Alan laid out a town with properties all along the bank of the river, a market place near the river crossing, a church close by, and large plots of building land on the east side of the Market Place. Until Boston Dock was built in the 1880s the port of Boston was the river through the town centre, with ships tying up at the wharfs and jetties on each

MARKET PLACE 1899 43296

WORMGATE 2005 B155701k (Neil Wright)

Picturesque and medieval, this curves to follow the old course of the River Witham.

bank. In 1142 Alan de Croun paid for a sluice to be erected across the river at Boston so that water could be released at low tide to flush the silt out of the river; but the first reference to a bridge here was in 1305 when lords of the manors on each bank were allowed to charge tolls to be used for its repair. Since then the bridge has been replaced every 100 years or

so; until 1807 the site was a few yards north of the present bridge.

There are no Norman buildings standing in Boston, but you can still follow the street pattern laid out over 900 years ago. Medieval towns were small, and eastern Boston was a long strip including the Market Place, South End, and Wormgate/Witham Place (originally Witham Gate). On the inland side of the town was a drain called the Barditch which was probably cut not long after the town was created. The line of Barditch is marked on a map of Boston published in

HIGH STREET 1899 43300

BESIDE THE RIVER 1899 43302

BARGATE GREEN 1890 26069

DOLPHIN LANE 2005 B155702k (Neil Wright)

In medieval times, this lane led to the fields east of the town on both sides of Main Ridge.

1887 by the Ordnance Survey, and in some places can still be followed on the ground today. The western part of the town was even smaller, including High Street south to Doughty Quay, and going north as far as the modern police station. Some lanes close to the Town Bridge still follow medieval lines, but those nearer to the modern St Botolph's footbridge were swept away in the 1960s. The only medieval extensions beyond these two core areas were Wide Bargate (originally two lanes with a green between them) and a few buildings in east Boston just outside the southern end of the town.

Around the built-up part of medieval Boston were common fields extending to the parish boundaries, and Boston people also had rights of common on the fens. Commoners could put horses, cattle, sheep and geese out to pasture on the fen, take fish from its waters, cut reeds for thatch and dig turf for fuel. Those rights over the fens were shared with many other villages on the townlands and the southern Wolds. People living in Boston east of the river had rights over the East, West and Wildmore Fens (which covered 40,000 acres in all), and those living west of the river shared rights over Holland Fen (22,000 acres). The fields within Boston parish would originally have been big open fields with individual names, and Broadfield Lane probably indicates one of those old names; at some time before 1545 these open fields were divided into individual enclosures or small fields that were built over in the 18th, 19th and, in York Street, 20th centuries.

SKIRBECK, ST NICHOLAS'S CHURCH 1893 32080

This bridge was built in 1807 and lasted until 1913; the medieval bridge was a few yards further north.

In 1086 the Domesday Book listed two churches in Skirbeck, one of which would be the original St Nicholas's Church and the other the Norman predecessor of St Botolph's. A separate parish was carved out for St Botolph's leaving Skirbeck as two bits, one on each bank of the Haven. The boundary between Boston and Skirbeck followed old streams that have since dried up, but the winding lane called Robin Hood's Walk still marks the old boundary at the north end of the town. There was, no doubt, hostility between the people of this new town, associated with the new foreign ruling class, and the fiercely independent descendants of Vikings and Saxons in the neighbouring villages. The town took its name from the parish church, and was variously called St Botolph's or Botolph'stown, though the spelling could vary. It was sometimes shortened to Boston, and after 1400 the original names were hardly every used.

Alan the Red had a manor house in the Mart Yard, which is now the front yard of the Grammar School. The manor house was behind what is now the school's library. For

A RIVER VIEW 1890 26067

most of Boston's medieval history there was no resident lord to interfere in day-to-day activities; local people were largely left to their own devices in the running of the town. The manor house was never a significant residence for Alan or those lords who came after him, and it soon fell into ruin. Boston had no self-government at this time, but the main official of the Honour of Richmond was the bailiff, who was often a local merchant living in Boston. One of the manor's main buildings was Gysor's Hall at the north end of South Square, on the site of Haven Villas and near to the centre of things where the Bailiff could keep an eye on what was going on. He collected tolls from all shipping entering the port and this, together with the profits from the markets and the fair, went to the lord.

In 1089, Alan the Red died. In his will he left the church of St Botolph to the Abbey of St Mary of York, who then received the income due to the church and appointed the parish priests. In 1098, the abbey founded a small priory in Boston where their priests lived during almost 400 years until the abbey gave up St Botolph's. It is believed the priory was on the north side of the churchyard, perhaps part of the modern car park in front of the Sessions House.

900 years ago international trade was much smaller than now as European countries produced most of what they needed, and there were few people who could afford to buy luxury goods. Nowadays we think of fairs as swings, roundabouts and other amusements but medieval fairs were really trade fairs with amusements added. Buyers

Fact File

In the Middle Ages fairs were mainly trading events to which people came long distances to buy and sell goods, and Boston fair became one of the most important in Europe. It was one of the main places where wool, the biggest export of medieval England, was bought and sold. It was so important that one year the courts in London closed so that merchants could attend Boston Fair.

and sellers had to meet face-to-face to strike bargains, and fairs were where they did it. England was good at producing wool, and Flanders, part of modern-day Belgium, was good at making that wool into quality cloth, so they were the chief commodities traded at Boston fair. Lincolnshire was one of the main areas producing wool, so Boston became the main port for exporting it to Europe.

The largest producers of wool included the Cistercian abbeys of Yorkshire and Lincolnshire, and they and other monasteries acquired houses in Boston that they could use when they came to sell their wool at the fair. The Cistercian order first arrived in England in 1132 when Fountains and Rievaulx Abbeys were founded in Yorkshire. The order looked for remote locations and soon set up houses on the fen edge near Boston, at Revesby in 1142 and Swineshead in 1148. The name of Fountain Lane in Boston still indicates the part of Wormgate where Fountains Abbey owned several buildings.

When the wool was sold, the agents for the noble and monastic producers had cash in their hands to spend on essentials and luxury goods for their masters. So Boston fair, first mentioned in 1125, became one of the most important in Europe as people traded not only wool and woollen cloth but other items such as lead from Derbyshire (used on the roofs of churches and castles), salt from the Lincolnshire coast (for preserving food), luxury cloth, wine, furs, leather, spices, falcons, wax, and more mundane goods such as timber, iron and stockfish. By 1203-04, the tax returns on merchants' goods in ports listed Boston at £781 - only a little less than London at £837. In 1218, the fair was said to last eight days but, by 1330, it ran from June until December. In about 1287 a gang led by Robert Chamberlain raided the fair, and set fire to buildings to distract attention while they looted the town. It was said that molten gold ran down the streets. Chamberlain was captured and hanged but didn't name any of his gang.

Medieval Boston was at its most prosperous in the late 13th and early 14th centuries, and the port was alive with foreign merchants and sailors such as those of the Hanseatic League of north German cities. The League dominated trade in northern Europe and the Baltic and, by 1260, some of its merchants had established a riverside depot in Boston, close to where the General Hospital was later built (now South Terrace). Hanseatic merchants

BLACKFRIARS THEATRE c1965 B155092

The Dominican friary was founded in 1222, and this is part of their later buildings, now used as the Blackfriars Theatre and Arts Centre.

were a dominant presence in Boston for the next 200 years or more and, after 1260, few other merchants from northern Europe visited Boston. They built their depot outside the town as a measure of greater security.

By the 1280s a third of all wool exports from England went out of Boston and, in 1300, nearly two million litres of wine came into the port. By 1332 Boston was the fourth wealthiest provincial town in England with a population of about 5,000. In 1330, a new aqueduct was built to bring in fresh water and, in 1347, the townspeople were temporarily allowed to elect a captain and mayor. This was the peak of Boston's medieval prosperity, and merchants founded guilds and friaries and started the construction of the great parish church that still dominates the town. The friars represented a new religious ideal, going to the people, in contrast to the contemplative and solitary life of the monasteries. The first friary in Boston had been founded by the Dominicans in 1222, and part of their later building is now the Blackfriars Theatre in Spayne Lane. In 1268, merchants of the Hansa helped establish a Franciscan friary close to the lanes still called Greyfriars Lane and White Cross Lane. Wisselus Smalenburg, whose tombstone of Tournai marble is now in St Botolph's Church, was originally buried in the Franciscan friary church in 1340. The Carmelite friars arrived in the reign of King Edward I, and acquired five acres of land on the west side of the river in 1293, perhaps near Doughty Quay, and built a friary there. Finally the Augustinian friars arrived in 1317, and got a licence to build in Skirbeck Road.

The same new religious feeling also led to the founding of guilds which, in Boston, were predominantly religious bodies with a strong social element. St Mary's Guild, formed in 1260, was the first in Boston, and for nearly 300 years was the main power in the town. Its hall was rebuilt in the 1390s, and is still in use as the town's museum after a major refurbishment at the start of the 21st century. The Guild had land not only in and around Boston but also in other counties in England. A number of other Guilds followed, including the Corpus Christi Guild founded in 1335 by Gilbert Alilaunde - its hall was near the river and might be the timber-frame building in South Street now called Shodfriars Hall; it was newer than St Mary's but was elite and aristocratic - a rich man's club. Its members included bishops, nobility, even royalty, in its 200-year history.

As Boston did not have a chartered Corporation for local government, the guilds could also serve as a forum for local people to discuss and promote town affairs. At least five guilds were large enough to own property in and around the town, and to have their own halls; a number of them jointly supported a grammar school in the town near the present vicarage in Wormgate. Each guild had a chapel in St Botolph's Church and contributed towards the maintenance of the church, and some also had a chapel in their own hall. The guilds employed priests to say Mass for the souls of deceased members of the guild; they owned candles, vestments and plate for religious use, and took part in the religious processions of the Catholic calendar. The guilds also owned

THE TOWN HALL 1893 32073

The Guild of St Mary (formed in 1260) built this hall c1390. It is now the town's museum.

In 1506 the Guild of St Mary in Boston sent a deputation to Rome to try to get more privileges for their members from Pope Julius II. They were advised that the best way to get the Pope's attention was to approach him as he came back from hunting. They sang a three-man glee, and then offered him a 'Jelly Junket', which was a sort of sweet pudding. They were successful, and got 500 years of pardon for those members of their guild whose subscriptions were paid up.

relics of saints, and were a centre of pilgrimage. Altogether, there were about fourteen guilds in Boston, though some were probably just formed to help fund-raising for the rebuilding of St Botolph's Parish Church.

Another important establishment in medieval Boston was run by the Order of St John, also called the Knights Hospitalers, who were a medieval 'good cause'. In about 1230 they had been given St Leonard's almshouses in Skirbeck (which were near Hospital Bridge), and looked after a number of people there for 300 years. Then by 1281, the Order had a second and more important

site in Boston. They founded a church, dedicated to St John, just outside the Barditch in Skirbeck Road, with almshouses attached to it that continued in use even after the Reformation.

The original Norman parish church of Boston had been provided by the lord of the manor but, 200 years later, the parishioners decided to replace it with a much grander building that reflected local pride and prosperity. Dame Margery (or Margaret) Tilney laid the foundation stone in 1309, and placed £5 on it. Throughout the following century work proceeded steadily on the massive new church, which represented the latest in style and technology. The very best craftsmen and materials were employed; large quantities of good stone were brought in from the Barnack quarries near Stamford and carved on site. Work began at the east end and continued westward. Remarkably slender pillars and soaring arches gave the

SHODFRIARS HALL 1889 22274

nave and chancel a new open feel, and the nave included a new feature - a series of fourteen windows at clerestory level. The main part of the church was completed by 1390, then the chancel was extended by a further two bays and the choir stalls put in place. There was no tower - that was to come later. The interior of the church would have looked quite different from how it does today, with screens around the guild chapels and in the chancel arch. Over the screen in the chancel arch was a huge Cross, and on the wall above that was a vivid painting of the Last Judgement. Everywhere were bright colours, statues, candles, the smell of incense and the chanting of priests at the numerous altars.

During the 14th century, Boston started several centuries of decline. As less cloth was produced in Flanders and more in England, wool exports were much reduced. The wool trade through Boston had reached its peak in 1283, and then went downhill. The constant dangers from piracy in the English Channel and North Sea became much more serious after the outbreak of the Hundred Years' War in 1337. The wine trade was reduced, and Gascon merchants involved in that trade seem to have deserted Boston in favour of the southern ports of London, Plymouth, Exeter and Bristol. The wool staple was transferred from Lincoln in 1369, and that created more jobs for leading Boston merchants but did not

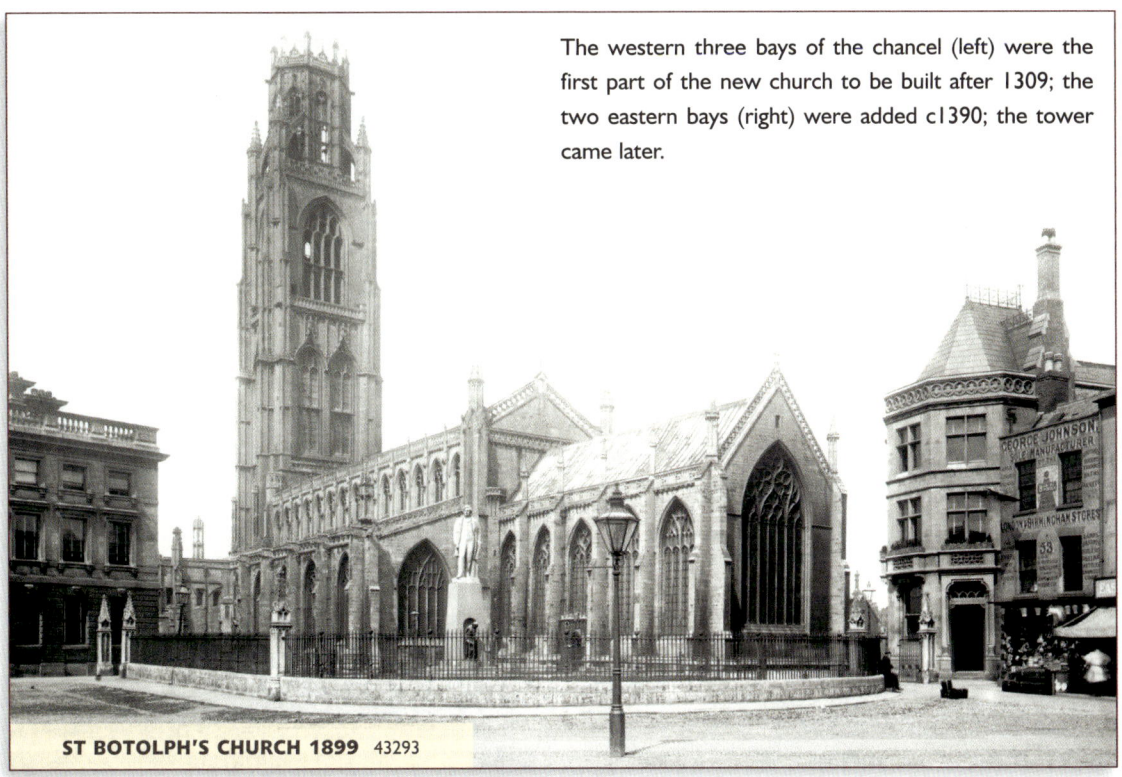

The western three bays of the chancel (left) were the first part of the new church to be built after 1309; the two eastern bays (right) were added c1390; the tower came later.

ST BOTOLPH'S CHURCH 1899 43293

THE CHURCH 1893 32068

THE CHURCH 1889 22269x

stop the long-term decline. Italian merchants stopped coming to Boston, and luxury goods were no longer available at the fair. The silting of the Fossdyke and the Witham at Boston also impeded the use of the harbour. By 1400, there were few foreign merchants at Boston Fair. It is said that most Hanseatic merchants stopped coming to Boston after one of them was killed in a fight during the reign of King Edward IV (1461-83); the last one is said to have visited Boston in 1518. However, Boston continued to serve as the market town for the villages round about, and continued to handle coastal traffic.

When we look at St Botolph's we see an ancient gothic building, and it is hard to think that it did not get its present appearance until the very end of the medieval period. Boston was no longer as rich as it had been, so it took longer to build the tower than to build the church itself. Begun around 1430, it was not completed until about 1520, just a few years before the Reformation. The tower is the tallest on a parish church in England,

and because of its height at 272 feet, and the imposing scale of the whole building, St Botolph's is often mistaken for a cathedral. It is a remarkable testimony to the skill of medieval masons that the tower still stands despite being so close to a tidal river. The top part of the tower is called a 'lantern', which refers to its shape, not to a medieval lighthouse with a fire inside its lantern! The name 'Boston Stump' only seems to have

THE CHURCH 1890 26734

been used for the last 200 years or so, and the name was probably intended as an insult to upset Boston people, who are justifiably proud of their church tower.

During 1348-49, England was devastated by the Black Death that killed a great many people. We do not have details as to how many died in Boston but, as a major port, it would have suffered as much as anywhere else. We know that the years after the Black Death were stressful for the Corpus Christi Guild which had no new admissions for a few years, but then it grew and peaked in 1392-1402. From 1490-1510 there was a fall in recruitment to that guild, reflecting the economic decline of Boston, but the

RICHARD FLEMING

Richard Fleming (died 1431) was rector of Boston from 1408 to 1419, when he became Bishop of Lincoln. He became a leading member of the Catholic Church in England and was part of delegations to Church Councils in Europe. In 1414 he attended the Council of Constance and was appointed papal chamberlain, and returned to England as an envoy of the Pope. Fleming was in Italy again in 1419 when the Bishop of Lincoln died, and he was consecrated to the vacant post in the cathedral at Florence. He still played a part in local affairs, being Alderman of the Corpus Christi Guild in Boston in 1412-14 and in 1426. Fleming also founded Lincoln College at Oxford.

Fact File

It is said that Boston Stump, the tower of the parish church of St Botolph is 'built on wool'. Some people think this is because sacks of wool were thrown into the foundation pit when the tower was built. This is not so. In fact, it means that the tower was paid for from the profits made by the merchants importing and exporting wool and other goods through the medieval port of Boston.

members did include Margaret Beaufort, the mother of King Henry VII. In the late Middle Ages, many people were obsessed with death and purgatory. Guilds were the focus for this general increase in popular piety and pilgrimages; in Boston they sustained both the parish church and the vitality of religious life. Their religious processions on saints' days were very elaborate by the late medieval period. In 1518, St Mary's Guild paid for a Noah's Ark to be carried by eight men in a procession that also had banners, crosses, torches and musicians.

St Mary's Guild supported a choir in the chancel of the parish church, and its high quality is demonstrated by attempts in 1524 and 1525 by members of the King's own Chapel Royal to conscript the best boys and men for the service of the crown. Some historians suggest that, by the 1530s, the guilds were more important for their social distinction and influence; but in the early 16th century, Boston guilds were still receiving bequests for priests to celebrate Mass for the souls of the departed. The guilds also supported a school, provided almshouses for poor people, and helped in other public works such as the maintenance of river banks and the town bridge, and their increasing participation in municipal affairs made it easy for them to support the creation of a new Corporation to run Boston in 1545.

Goodbarn's Yard to the north of St Botolph's Church was the site of the medieval grammar school, and is now the site of the modern vicarage. The name, Goodbarn's Yard, has also been taken by the public house north of the vicarage.

THE CHURCH 1890 26071x

THE FORMER RODNEY AND HOOD PUBLIC HOUSE, 2005 B155703k (Neil Wright)

Demolition of adjoining buildings has revealed that, at 35 High Street, the former Rodney and Hood public house (from c1794 to c1913) is a 15th-century building, with a timber frame next to the street and a brick structure to the rear.

When the Abbey of St Mary of York decided to end its involvement with St Botolph's Church in 1478, control of the parish church passed to the King and then, in 1482, to the Order of St John. The Knights moved from Skirbeck Road to a site next to the parish church. After 1482, St John's Church slowly deteriorated; its stone was used to repair St Botolph's and the town bridge, and the last part of it was demolished in 1626. The almshouses at Skirbeck Road continued in use until about 1726, by which time the road next to them had been named St John's Road, as it is today. The large site continued as a burial ground until the 1850s, and is now a pleasant recreational ground with fine trees.

You can still see a number of fine buildings to remind us of Boston's medieval heyday, most notably St Botolph's Church, St Mary's guildhall and Blackfriars. Then there are the brick-built Hussey Tower and Rochford Tower, both c1450-60 and inspired by Tattershall Castle, which was started in 1431; the timber and brick house at 35 High Street was also built in this period. The timber-framed Shodfriars Hall (page 22) and Pescod Hall (both 15th-century) have been much altered over the centuries; 25 High Street (15th century) and the Church Quay building (16th-century) are more authentic, though their timber-frames would have been decently covered in the past. The side wall of 61 High Street, next to Haven Bridge, reveals that probably quite a few later-looking buildings have timber frames buried within them; for instance, those in the narrow passage next to 19 Market Place.

ORDNANCE SURVEY MAP OF BOSTON 1887

IT IS STRANGE how some bits of history get changed into myths. Some people think that the Pilgrim Fathers sailed from Boston in the 'Mayflower', and founded the United States. It is even said that someone's grandmother can remember seeing the 'Mayflower' sailing out of Boston. Sadly it's not true. Some of the Pilgrim Fathers did go to Boston, and stayed longer than they intended. But they didn't sail anywhere from Boston; the 'Mayflower'

THE HUSSEY TOWER 1893 32077

was never there, and someone's granny must have been about 400 years old to have seen anything of the Pilgrim Fathers!

The real story of Boston's involvement with the founding of the United States in the early

This was built about 1485, and later acquired by Lord Hussey. On the right is the Grammar School of 1567, now the school library.

1600s is less well-known but is even more remarkable, and has had a profound effect on the character of the world's most powerful nation. Our Boston could well be said to have influenced the strong Puritanical element in American society. An odd thing is that 100 years before Boston sent Puritan settlers to America, in the early 1500s, most people in Boston were good Roman Catholics. So how did Boston change to a Puritan town?

King Henry VIII is the one who started the chain of events that were to have such a profound effect on Boston and the wider world. Henry VIII's separation from Catherine of Aragon in the 1530s caused more pain to more people than most divorces. Because the Pope would not let him have a divorce, Henry broke with Rome, and made himself the Head of the Church in England, although he remained a Catholic. Once in control, Henry started to reform the Church and, most notoriously, closed the monasteries and seized their riches for himself. In the turmoil that followed, local men, including Lord Hussey, lost their lives - but overall the leading citizens of Boston actually benefited.

As usual when faced by drastic change, some people objected, some welcomed it, and some did not think it went far enough. Most people did not mind the break with Rome (there was Euro-scepticism then too) but, in Lincolnshire and elsewhere, many people wanted the monasteries, friaries, churches and services to continue as before. The elderly Lord Hussey, whose Boston home included the brick tower still called Hussey Tower, tended to favour the old ways but, by the 1530s, he was Lord Lieutenant and the King's chief representative in the county so he could not be openly hostile. By the end of August 1536, the King's Commissioners had closed 36 of the 52 monasteries in Lincolnshire, evicted the monks and nuns, and seized their property. The gentry might not have resisted the changes but the ordinary people decided to do something about it before it was too late.

What they did is called the 'Lincolnshire Rising'. It started in October 1536 in Louth, Horncastle and Caistor from where people marched to Lincoln, gathering others as they went. The worst incident was when Dr Raynes, Chancellor of Lincoln Cathedral, was dragged from Old Bolingbroke to Horncastle on Wednesday 4 October, and clubbed to death by the mob, encouraged by a considerable number of clergy. Word spread around the county and, on that Thursday and Friday, people from surrounding villages made their way into Boston. Anthony Irby, whose new house was on the west bank opposite the Stump, left town and took 150 men to join the royal forces but other gentlemen were forced to swear to be true to God, the King, the commons and the commonwealth. Some of the Boston crowd went to Lincoln. At the same time, Lord Hussey apparently tried to mediate between the rebels and the King's forces and, when told he should be opposing them, he left his Sleaford home in disguise and went to Nottingham.

A leading part in suppressing this ineffectual rebellion was played by Charles Brandon, Duke of Suffolk, who was a close friend of the King and married to his sister, Mary. The Duke had a succession of marriages, and his last was to Lady Katherine Willoughby de Eresby, the heiress to a vast Lincolnshire estate that included Grimsthorpe where he built a castle. For a brief period the Duke played an important, if largely forgotten, part in the history of Boston. The rebels had sent a letter to the King listing their grievances, and his reply was read out in the Chapter House of Lincoln Cathedral on 10th October. In it, he famously referred to the county as 'one of the most brute and beastly in the realm'. The reply caused quarrels and divisions and, the following day, the gentry decided to capitulate to the Duke of Suffolk, who was on his way from London leading some of the king's forces. The gentry also advised the ordinary people to go home, and the government were told that 'the township of Boston with others have fled home again within these two days and I suppose the rest will flee shortly'.

But the rebels weren't allowed to get away with it. King Henry was intolerant of anyone who opposed him, and determined to make an example of Lincolnshire. The Duke of Suffolk arrived in Lincoln, and evidence was taken from the leaders of the common people. On 14 November, the Duke announced a general pardon for all those he had released, but those still in prison suffered the death penalty. Some were hanged in February 1537, and 32 more in March. For his failure to resist the rebels, Lord Hussey was found guilty of treason and beheaded in Lincoln in July 1537. As well as the executions, there were fines on the county and towns, and Boston had to pay £50. This showed that rebellion was futile, and most people had to accept the new order.

JOHN TAVERNER

John Taverner (1495-1545) was a composer of sacred music in the years before the Reformation. In 1524, he was a member of the Choir of Tattershall College in Lincolnshire, and was appointed by Cardinal Wolsey in 1526 as the first instructor of the choristers at Cardinal College, Oxford (now Christ Church College). In 1530 he joined the famous choir of St Botolph's Church, Boston. By 1537 he had left the choir but remained at Boston, and was a member of the Corpus Christi Guild. He became one of the first Aldermen of Boston Corporation. Most of his music was written during his time at Oxford. His life and work inspired an opera 'Taverner' by Peter Maxwell Davies, first performed at Covent Garden in 1972.

Many people in Boston accepted the changes, or at least said they had done so. The composer, John Taverner, had moved to Boston in 1530 to take over the famous choir supported by St Mary's Guild in the chancel of the Stump. He later became a reformer, and 'repented him that he had made songs to Popish ditties in the time of his blindness'. In the autumn of 1538, he reported that the great cross that used to hang in the chancel arch had been burned on a market day in the Market Place, and that 'the sermon of the Black Friar at the burning has done much good'. One friar might be embracing reform but, like the rest of his brethren, he did not know what the future held. Two years later the friary was suppressed, and its buildings (of which part is now the Blackfriars Theatre) were granted to the Duke of Suffolk. But the Boston guilds continued for a few more years. Taverner joined the Corpus Christi Guild in 1537, and was its chamberlain in 1543.

During the 1530s and 1540s King Henry acquired a vast amount of real estate in Boston. It came from Lord Hussey, about 20 former monasteries and priories, the four friaries in the town, and the Order of St John that he suppressed in 1540. Quite a lot of this, including the Dominican friary and the Knights Hospitalers' property in the town, was given to the Duke of Suffolk whose preferred residence in Lincolnshire was Tattershall Castle, just a few miles north of Boston, which the King had given him in April 1537. The Duke helped some leading men of Boston to start negotiations to form a Corporation which would acquire this property and other rights and privileges in the town. Then in 1545 the Duke died, and so did King Henry's illegitimate son, the Duke of Richmond; their property in Boston, including the manor of Hallgarth, passed back to the crown. The leading men of Boston agreed with the King that, in return for a payment of £1,646 15s 4d, the King would grant them a charter making the town a municipal borough, and also giving it this property and other privileges.

FROM THE FERRY 1893 32063x

Boston Corperation, formed 1545, took over the Mart Yard and the buildings shown here were later built between the Mart Yard and the Haven.

PESCOD SQUARE 2005 B155704k (Neil Wright)

One of Boston's oldest buildings is 15th-century Pescod Hall, part of which still survives and gives its name to a new shopping precinct.

Boston Corporation came into existence on 14 May 1545. The charter not only gave them the lordship of the manor of Hallgarth and a large collection of property, but also the right to collect tolls belonging to the manor, and the right (previously held by the Order of St John) to appoint the Vicar of Boston. The Corporation kept the right to choose the two MPs for the town until 1640. It remained an oligarchy until 1835 when a major reform allowed it to be elected by some of the townspeople. It stayed that way until 1974 when a new borough council took over the town and surrounding rural district.

Many towns had corporations like this, but in Boston there was an unusual further development. On 12 July 1545 the heads of the five incorporated guilds, four of whom were aldermen or councillors of the new Corporation, voluntarily handed over all the lands and goods of the guilds of St Mary, the Holy Trinity, St Peter and St Paul, St George and Corpus Christi. This meant that initially the Corporation employed a large number of priests and other officials to carry on the religious duties of the former guilds. Nicholas Robinson had resigned his position as Warden of St Mary's Guild to become the first Mayor of the new Corporation on 1 June 1545. The hall of St Mary's Guild became the Corporation's headquarters, and is still in use today as the town's museum.

When King Henry died in 1547, a more Protestant regime was imposed under his son Edward VI. An Act of that year abolished guilds, and the new Boston Corporation lost the property it had got from the guilds.

In 1551 the property of the Corpus Christi Guild ended up with Lord Clinton, and then the Marquis of Northampton claimed that of the other four guilds, though he handed back to the Corporation the guildhall and other goods and chattels, but not the guilds' land and property. The Corporation stopped all the duties they had taken over from the guilds; over a number of years, it held a vast sale of chapel furnishings, plate, hangings, vestments and other items of the town's medieval heritage. In the following centuries, medieval buildings were dismantled to provide stone and timber for repairs to the town bridge, sea banks, riverside wharves, and the parish church itself. Very few buildings remain that were built before 1545.

The Catholic Queen Mary came to the throne in 1553, and Boston Corporation obtained a new charter granting them the remaining unsold guild lands. Only about a quarter of them remained, and these 'Erection Lands' were to pay for two priests at the church, a master and usher at the grammar school, and four bedesmen. At first the grammar school continued in its old building in Wormgate (on the site of the modern vicarage) but in 1567 it moved to a new building in the Mart Yard, which is now the school library. The only guildhall that the Corporation got back was St Mary's, which continued as their headquarters, including the town's courts, until the 19th century. It has undergone drastic changes (eg sash windows added in 1722) so it is difficult to imagine what the medieval room arrangements were.

Queen Mary's efforts to restore Catholicism had driven many Protestants abroad, including the Boston-born John Foxe. His 'Book of Martyrs' (published 1554, 2nd edition 1570)

THE GRAMMAR SCHOOL, THE SOUTH END 2005 B155705k (Neil Wright)

This was built in 1567, with smaller Victorian additions on each side.

became crucially important in the debate to define England's religion and character. After the Bible, it was the most read book in the English language. When Queen Elizabeth I came to the throne, she achieved a religious settlement between Catholic and Protestant beliefs; but dissent grew and Boston went down the Puritan road to 'purify' the Church of England of remaining Catholic practices. In 1590, the vicar persuaded the Corporation to destroy the rood at the entrance to the chancel, and the last Elizabethan vicar, Mr Wooll, refused to wear his surplice, a traditional priest's vestment, and sat on it.

Boston was run by the new Corporation from 1545, but they could not do much to raise the town out of the economic depression of the previous 200 years or so. In the 1520s, it had been only 22nd in the valuation of English towns, and its position continued to fall. Queen Elizabeth later granted it a charter for Admiralty jurisdiction over the Wash, and that proved a good source of income. But the river was silting up and the port was in a bad way. In 1584, the Mayor told Lord Burghley that the only goods to leave the port that year were 260 quarters of barley-malt. Incidentally, the Mayor of Boston can still claim the title of 'Admiral of the Wash'.

Boston reached its peak as a centre of Protestantism in the first half of the 17th century. From 1612 to 1633, the vicar was the young, learned, zealous and devout John Cotton who attracted many leading Protestants to the town with his vigorous Calvinisim. He was a powerful preacher, and none could resist his influence. Others who shared his

SKIRBECK, ST NICHOLAS'S CHURCH 1890 26083

The chancel of St Nicholas's Church was destroyed by a flood in 1558 and was not replaced until 1908. This photograph shows the blocked arch at the end of the nave before the new chancel was built.

beliefs came to Boston to be near him, either living in the town or travelling there to hear his sermons. The new pulpit built in his time is still in use today. When King James I came to the throne in 1603, the Church of England had started to be less tolerant of dissent, and some Protestants came to believe that they would have to leave the country to worship in the way they wanted. Boston did play a part - but only a minor one - in the first Puritan settlement of New England. A group from north Nottinghamshire made an attempt to sail from Boston to the Netherlands in 1607, but were betrayed, and put on trial in the court in Boston Guildhall. All but seven were acquitted, and were probably sent to the town gaol on the site where the Ingram Memorial is now. They later sailed from Immingham to the Netherlands and in 1620 some of them, known as the Pilgrim Fathers, made their famous voyage to Massachusetts, but the Boston link with America was another adventure altogether.

There is no historical link between New York and the city of York in England, but the two Bostons, of Lincolnshire and Massachusetts, USA, are umbilically linked - they are mother and daughter. A group of committed, rich, powerful, educated people decided to emigrate as a group to reproduce their old town on a new continent, and in an idealised form free from the restraints they had suffered in the old world. Their dream to create a committed, rich, powerful, educated

THE TOWN HALL CELLS 1899 43299

In 1607 these cells in Boston Guildhall contained some of the people later known as the Pilgrim Fathers while awaiting trial; the steps up to the courtroom are on the right.

new Boston was achieved. Within a short time of arriving in America, they established not only a grammar school (which still exists) but also the foundations of Harvard University. Men from old Boston dominated the government and church of Massachusetts for about 50 years. Their colony became the richest one in British North America, and to this day Boston is the capital of the Commonwealth of Massachusetts. These are not just two places that share the same name - it was men from one Boston who created the other.

So long as the Puritans of Boston were safe they felt no need to emigrate. That changed in 1627 when William Laud, Bishop of London, started more intense efforts to impose High Church uniformity. An exodus was first planned in 1628 in the West Country but the following year, when the Massachusetts Bay Company was formed, the leadership

had moved to the area around Boston. They already knew the name of Massachusetts, as New England had recently been mapped and named by the Lincolnshire-born explorer Captain John Smith. At the heart of the planned emigration was the household of Theophilus Clinton-Fiennes. Born in 1600, the young 4th Earl of Lincoln inherited the title in 1619, and his inspiration was the Revd John Cotton. The Earl's main home was Tattershall Castle but he also had a town house in Wide Bargate, Boston, where his three sisters had spent much of their early lives. These sisters each married men who were to play important parts in the exodus. The Earl stayed in England and during the Civil War raised a regiment for Parliament.

Among the leaders of the exodus were Thomas Dudley and his son-in-law Simon Bradstreet. Dudley lived in Boston and was Lord Lincoln's steward. Other emigrants were: Alderman Thomas Leverett and his young son John; the Rev Samuel Whiting, Rector of Skirbeck; Richard Bellingham, MP; Thomas James, headmaster of the Grammar School; Edmund Quincy of Fishtoft; and William Coddington who moved to Boston from Grantham by 1627 and, in 1638, was to become one of the founders of the Rhode Island colony. Altogether, it is estimated that 250 of the 3,000 people then living in Boston emigrated to New England before 1640, and sixteen of them were graduates of Cambridge University. Related as they were by marriage and old association, these Boston men dominated the new colony for two generations. Five of them were governors for several years, and eight were among the founders or early overseers of Harvard. It was because of the dominance of this group from the original Boston that the site chosen for the capital of the new colony was also named 'Boston'.

The first emigrants from Boston sailed in a fleet from Southampton in 1630. One ship carrying the Rev Isaac Johnson and his wife, a sister of Lord Lincoln, was renamed 'Arbella' in her honour. Also on that ship were Thomas Dudley and his daughter, Anne Bradstreet, who was to be the first American poet to have her work published. In 1633 the Revd John Cotton and several more families of his congregation sailed in the 'Griffin', and Cotton's influence in the new colony was so great that he was referred to as 'the unmitred pope of a pope-hating commonwealth'. Whatever he said from his pulpit in the New England church soon became an order of the court, and the persecuted became the persecutors - for instance, a kiss on a Sunday was punished by a spell in the stocks. Cotton kept in touch with his old parish and, in 1650, expressed gratitude for their continued help to him.

The top person in the government of the colony of Massachusetts was the Governor. In the early years of the colony this post was held by four men from the original Boston contingent, and, when not Governor, they usually held some other high post. These four men were Thomas Dudley, Simon Bradstreet, Richard Bellingham and John Leverett. Bellingham shocked everyone by marrying his ward, the beautiful Penelope Pelham (already betrothed to another man) without any service at all, except their own prayers.

BOSTON MEN RAN MASSACHUSETTS FOR 60 YEARS

In the 1630s, a twelfth of Boston's population emigrated to the colony of Massachusetts, and several Boston men held one or other of the top jobs in the colony for the next 60 years. They included Thomas Dudley, Simon Bradstreet, Richard Bellingham and John Leverett. Their spiritual leader was the Revd John Cotton who was Vicar of Boston from 1612 until he emigrated in 1633. These men ran a Puritan colony, founded the famous Harvard University as a Puritan college, and introduced the Puritan ethics that are still such a strong element in the character of the American people. They named their main settlement 'Boston' after the town from which the leaders came.

Even while John Cotton and his congregation were moving to New England, the environment around the old Boston they left behind was undergoing drastic changes. Encouraged by King Charles I, some major landowners were draining the fens around the town, enclosing them and dividing them up amongst themselves. In 1631 Sir Anthony Thomas, and other 'Adventurers' as they called themselves, started to reclaim the East and West Fens north of Boston. The King himself commissioned work in Holland Fen to the west of the town, though he soon gave that job to Sir William Killigrew. At first the Adventurers seemed to have succeeded, building drains and sluices, fences and

Fact File

The Maud Foster Drain in east Boston was dug in 1568 to replace the old Scire Beck, and reduce flooding of the fens north of Boston. Richard Foster was a coal merchant and ship-owner and, when he died in 1563, his widow Maud carried on his business until her own death in 1581. Maud Foster had a coal store next to the Queen's Head (on the site of the Sam Newsom Music Centre), and she presumably had land (somewhere between Cowbridge and Hospital Bridge) through which the Maud Foster Drain was cut.

houses, and harvesting crops for a number of years. What we still have from that time are the South Forty Foot Drain, North Forty Foot Drain, and Anton's Gowt, named after Sir Anthony Thomas as the only lock linking the Witham to the northern fens.

Then the commoners rose up in their hundreds and destroyed fences, sluices, houses and crops, and drove the Adventurers off the vast common fens. Serious rioting broke out in April 1641, and when Sir Edward Heron, the new sheriff of the county, met other magistrates in Boston to consider the matter, the rioters confidently came to town. Two of the ringleaders were arrested but a huge crowd, said to be more than 1,000 people, surrounded the house where Sir Edward and the other county magistrates sheltered, and threatened to demolish it. The borough magistrates refused to help, so Sir Edward had to free the prisoners; as he and the

other justices left Boston, they were followed by a jeering crowd that threw stones and mud after them. This lack of support from the Boston magistrates for the Royalist Sir Edward was a reflection of the growing divide that soon broke into civil war. In May 1641 Lord Willoughby of Parham, Lord Lieutenant of Lincolnshire, was asked to use the militia against the fen rioters but declined to do so, saying 'the times were dangerous'. Local juries refused to indict rioters brought before them.

The English Civil Wars began on 22 August 1642 when King Charles I raised his standard at Nottingham. But in June, Lord Willoughby of Parham had already toured Lincolnshire to raise militia for Parliament; Boston was the first place to respond as the mayor and 100 well-armed and trained volunteers turned out to meet him. Sir Edward Heron was loyal to the King, and tried to commandeer horses in Skirbeck but was arrested by Sir Anthony Irby, one of Boston's MPs, and sent to London where he was tried for treason, and spent two years in the Tower. Sir Anthony raised a troop of dragoons with himself as captain and later that year took them into Yorkshire to join Lord Fairfax. In August 1642 some prominent Royalists who landed near Skegness were captured, together with goods belonging to Prince Rupert, and were sent by boat as prisoners from Boston to London. The King was furious and ordered no-one to aid or assist Boston, but no cavaliers dared to enter the town.

Boston was a crucial port on the frontier between the Royalist north and the Parliamentary stronghold of East Anglia.

Lincolnshire was fought over and changed hands a number of times but Boston was never attacked and always supported Parliament. Banks of earth were built as defences, presumably on the northern and western sides of the town, but none remain and unlike some other towns we do not have any plans of Boston's fortifications. The Corporation obtained some cannons in 1643, and they can still be seen in the guildhall though the frames and wheels they sit on are 19th-century.

The most dangerous time for the town was in late 1643. In August, the Royalist Duke of Newcastle captured most of Lincolnshire, and fortified Bolingbroke Castle and Wainfleet on the southern edge of the Wolds, capturing Lord Lincoln's home at Tattershall Castle in mid-August. Boston was full of Parliamentary troops and refugees, and morale must have been low as the town feared for its safety. Lord Willoughby of Parham had his headquarters in the town, and Oliver Cromwell's cavalry bivouacked in the Stump where they tethered their horses to the pillars, destroyed the font, smashed the remaining medieval glass and statues, and melted the memorial brasses for bullets.

On 9 October 1643, a Parliamentary army led by the Earl of Manchester left Boston via Stickford to start retaking Lincolnshire. They besieged Bolingbroke Castle, and Cromwell and Sir Thomas Fairfax defeated a Royalist force at the Battle of Winceby to the west of the castle. Cromwell's horse was killed under him but the charge was decisive and the battle short. This was the start of Cromwell's

THE CHURCH 1890 26073

spectacular career. Lord Manchester then went on to capture Lincoln.

From October 1643, Boston was under the command of military governors. The first was Edward King who managed to fall out with others on the Parliamentary side. Early in 1644, a Parliamentary assault on Newark provoked a counter attack by Prince Rupert who forced the Parliamentary army, including troops from Boston, to surrender. Boston again feared an attack by the Royalists, but Prince Rupert did not stay in Lincolnshire, and Parliament reasserted control of the county. Later that year, Royalists made further forays into the county until Colonel Edward Rossiter made the Parliamentary forces in the county effective enough to stop Boston fearing a Royalist attack.

In December 1644 Crowland was recaptured by Parliamentary infantry, led by Colonel Thomas Rainborowe; several officers in his regiment were returned New Englanders, including Captain John Leverett who had left the original Boston in 1633. Leverett later returned to Massachusetts, and gave many years' service to the Ancient and Honourable Artillery Company, becoming Major General of the forces of the colony, only resigning when he was elected Governor. Relative safety brought its own problems and, in July 1645, Boston Corporation complained that the garrison in the town had not been paid for months and was ready to mutiny. The inhabitants lodging the soldiers 'were so impoverished that they were no longer able to bear it'. The government's response was to have the defences surveyed to see if they could be reduced in size.

OLIVER CROMWELL USED THE STUMP AS STABLES

During the Civil War Boston was a stronghold of the Parliamentary forces, on the edge of their Eastern Association and facing the Royalist north. When most of Lincolnshire was held by the Royalists in 1643, Oliver Cromwell commanded the cavalry in the force defending Boston. He used the Three Tuns pub as his base in the Market Place at the corner of Church Lane. His troops took over the parish church, and their horses were fastened to rings in the pillars. Cromwell marched north with the army to fight a battle at Winceby near Bolingbroke Castle in the southern Wolds on 16th October. It was this battle that helped to make his reputation, and led to him becoming the best general on the Parliamentary side, and ultimately its leader.

The first phase of the Civil War came to an end when the Royalist garrison of Newark surrendered on 6 May 1646. In 1649 the Commonwealth government ordered the destruction of fortresses that might be used against it in a Royalist uprising, including Tattershall Castle, the home of Lord Lincoln who 20 years earlier had been involved in the emigration from Boston to Massachusetts. He was a Puritan who raised a regiment for Parliament but had not agreed with its more extreme views, and so was regarded with suspicion. He had friends in Boston, so the destruction of his castle was not total. It left the walls of the keep standing (which enabled it to be restored in 1912). In late December 1650, Boston's garrison was still maintained and comprised three infantry companies of 100 men each. All the weapons removed from Belvoir and Tattershall Castles were sent to an arsenal at Boston, and there was a garrison here until soon after the final defeat of King Charles II at Worcester on 3 September 1651. Some of the Royalists captured at the Battle of Dunbar were sent to Massachusetts; later in 1651, John Cotton wrote to Oliver Cromwell to say that their wounds and illnesses had been well attended, and they had been sold into slavery for just six or seven years rather than for life.

During the Commonwealth, Boston was once again in the doldrums, and its parish church was sadly neglected. Boston's Baptist community dates back to 1653 and is one of the oldest in the country. When the monarchy was restored in 1660, repairs were done to the parish church and, symbolically, a new font was installed and a central area of pews erected. Eight aldermen of Boston Corporation and eight of the common councillors who had supported the Commonwealth were removed. Bankes Anderson, lecturer of St Botolph's who didn't believe in infant baptism, lost his place, and set up a meeting-house in the town which is considered to be the foundation of later non-conformity here. Boston was not a flourishing port but a few merchants still made a good living, and there was enough trade to justify the building of a new Customs House on Packhouse Quay in 1725, which continued in use until 1983. The magnificent Fydell House dates from the same period.

PACKHOUSE QUAY, SOUTH STREET 2005
B155706k (Neil Wright)

PACKHOUSE QUAY 1899 43304

CHAPTER THREE

GEORGIAN AND VICTORIAN BOSTON

THE LAYOUT OF the town might be medieval but most of the buildings in and around the Market Place are more recent, being built of brick with grey slate roofs. Most were rebuilt when Boston was a boom town between 1770 and 1850. This is the period, from King George III to Queen Victoria, which had the most impact on the present appearance of its historic core. Nearly all the earlier buildings were swept away or had new fronts added. Boston must have been pretty rich and ambitious to undertake such major rebuilding. It grew into the biggest and liveliest town in Lincolnshire for a few years. Boston's affairs were affected by things happening elsewhere, but it was local people who saw the opportunities, and their decisions let Boston enjoy many years of prosperity. Fate helped Boston at this time, but booms are often followed by busts and, in 1848, the town saw the other side of the coin.

The sequence of events that were to transform Boston started in Holland Fen to the west of the town. The efforts to drain the local fens in the 1640s had not succeeded, but the issue would not go away, as the Adventurers had shown that it could be done. A century later the fens were transformed at last. The fens before enclosure were big open country. Holland Fen went from Fenside Road on the edge of Boston for about eight miles to East Heckington, and was also about eight miles from north to south. The East, West and Wildmore Fens ran into each other north of the town, and altogether were about twice as big as Holland Fen. On the open fens there were no farms or houses, no fields or

hedges, and the roads were tracks. There were lots of areas of water in the wet season, some quite large, but many of them dried up if there was a long, hot summer. The fens were not a pleasant place to live, in fact hardly anyone did live there permanently. Even people living on the edges of the fens were liable to suffer from ague and, into the 19th century, were using opium to relieve the pain.

But the fens were far from being a wasteland. They had many benefits for the cottagers with common rights who lived around them.

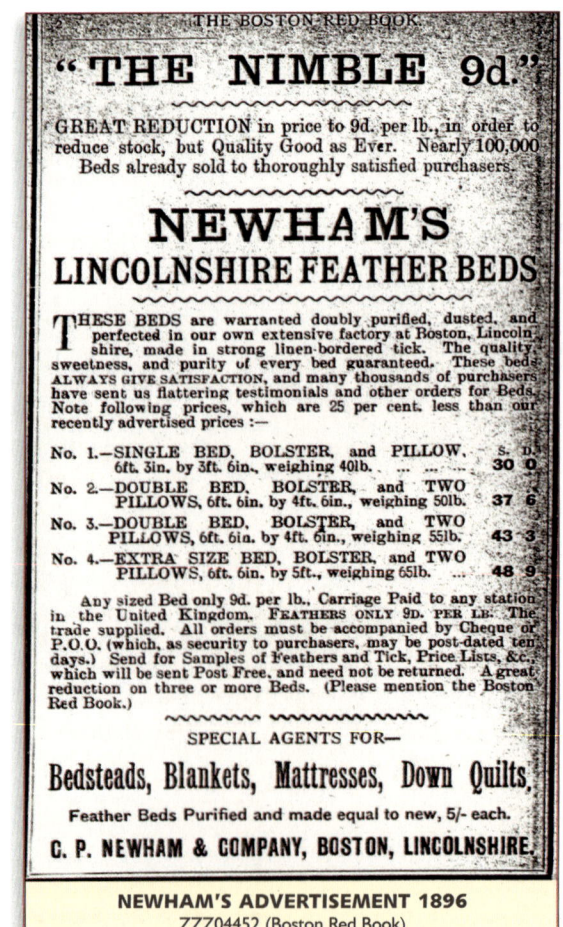

Commoners could gather thatch for roofs, cut rushes to strew on the floor, dig sods of turf for fuel, catch wildfowl, and fish in the numerous small lakes as well as putting cattle, sheep and horses out to graze. Then there were the geese, often referred to as the 'fenmen's treasure'; there were great flocks of them on the fens, and they could be plucked twice a year to provide quill pens for lawyers, and feathers for luxurious pillows and mattresses. In fact, the feather industry survived after enclosure, and is now represented by the firm 'Fogarty's of Boston'.

Landowners and farmers were experimenting with ways of improving the value of their land, and small fields were better than vast commons. In the 1760s,

agreement had been reached to straighten and embank the River Witham for navigation and improving the drainage of adjoining fens. The scheme was designed by the engineer John Grundy, with amendments agreed with Langley Edwards and John Smeaton. North of Boston a completely new channel for the Witham was built as far as Chapel Hill - twelve miles long - and a Grand Sluice was built just outside the town to prevent the tides going further inland and flooding the fens. The foundations of the Grand Sluice had been laid on 26 March 1764, and it was opened before a vast crowd on 3 October 1766. The project was immense as the new course of the river had to be dug out by hand, and the spoil removed by wheelbarrow, requiring lots

The Grand Sluice and the River Witham north of it were dry land until the new channel was dug in the 1760s.

THE SLUICE, BRIDGE AND RIVER c1955 B155064

THE RIVER 1893 32062

of navvies. In Boston it is difficult to see the old course of the river, but it went along the south side of Fydell Street, then turned north to go along the east side of Carlton Road until it reached the last house on Witham Bank West. The Grand Sluice was built in a pit in a field before the river was diverted.

Under Acts of Parliament Holland Fen was drained and divided between the parishes around it, and then each parish divided its part between everyone who had a share in the ownership of the fen or rights over it. Each person who got land in Holland Fen then put hedges around their own fields to enclose them. The poorer people only got small pieces of land that were not of much use to anyone - so they sold them to bigger landowners.

It took a number of years to carry out the process of dividing up the land, laying out roads, digging drains, planting thorn hedges, improving the land, and harvesting the crops from more and more fields. As in the 1640s, when enclosure had last been attempted, the fenmen resisted violently. The Act to drain Holland Fen was obtained in 1767 and, on 6 June 1768, a great crowd assembled at Hubbert's Bridge and marched into Boston. They scattered lawyer Draper's papers in the street, and then demonstrated outside the homes of Robert Barlow, a leading merchant, and Mr Tunnard and Mr Yerburgh who both lived in Frampton. A month later, the landowners hired some navvies to capture the mob's ringleaders, including 'Gentleman' Smith of Swineshead, but when the rioters met at Kirton Holme there were nearly a thousand of them, and the navvies thought better of it!

Four troops of the Scots Greys regiment were sent to Boston to prevent the rioters burning the town, but in the fen itself murder and mayhem continued for another five years. Robert Barlow and his brother-in-law William Garfit, another Boston merchant, each had coach horses poisoned and, as she sat by her fire, Mrs Barlow was shot in the head by a bullet aimed at her husband. Houses, barns and haystacks were set ablaze, and sheep maimed and killed, but the violence was of no avail. In 1769 the 22,000 acres of Holland Fen were divided between the ten parishes, with Boston getting 1,514 acres and, within

five years, eight of the parishes had divided their land and abolished common rights.

The East, West and Wildmore Fens to the north of Boston included lots of meres or lakes that were more difficult to drain. It would be an expensive job but 30 years later (during the Napoleonic wars) the price of grain and bread rose in England, and the potential profits made it worthwhile to undertake the drainage of those fens. This was completed by 1812 under a scheme devised by the great engineer John Rennie that included the widening of the Maud Foster Drain.

The River Witham improvements in the 1760s allowed boats to travel easily between Boston and Lincoln. As the Grand Sluice was a

THE WINDMILL c1965 B155096

THE WHARF, WAREHOUSE, AND GRAND SLUICE LOCK AT THE END OF THE WITHAM NAVIGATION 2005 B155707k (Neil Wright)

quarter of a mile north of the town, a new area developed, and became known as Witham Town. Boats carried passengers as well as goods on the river, and the great Barge Inn was built to cater for their needs. A few factories, an iron works, a woad mill, a boat yard and a rope walk were built in Witham Town, with workers' houses in Witham Green; later the Gas Works was built on the opposite bank.

Once Holland Fen had been enclosed, fields could be ploughed and fertilised to produce arable crops. John Wesley, the founder of Methodism, visited Boston in 1759, 1761 and 1780; in the latter year, he considered that the countryside had changed much for the better, and climbed the church tower to view for himself the fens that were now drained and converted into rich pasture and arable land. The cattle, sheep, horses and geese previously

reared on Holland Fen had been driven to market on their own feet; the new arable crops had to be harvested, put in carts, and shipped to their destinations by river or sea from Boston. For this town, the grain really was golden!

By the latter part of the 18th century, there was a growing demand for basic foods to feed the mouths of London and the industrial cities of England. The port of Boston became at least as busy as it had been in its medieval heyday, but its main business was now in grain and other food crops rather than the wool, cloth and luxury goods it had handled 500 years earlier. In 1815 young Samuel Leigh, newly arrived in Boston, wrote to tell his parents in Leicestershire that vast numbers of ships came to Boston. 'I can see the tops of the mast poles of the ships over the houses as

I walk the streets. They appear sometimes like a wood when the leaves are off when they are close together.'

Until the late 18th century the port and town of Boston was very quiet and, in 1760, its population was only about 3,470. But the growth of port traffic in the closing decade of the century needed workers, and young men were attracted to the town in great numbers. By 1801, the population of Boston was 5,926, or 6,465 if Skirbeck and Skirbeck Quarter are included. This population growth continued throughout the first half of the 19th century so that, by 1851, there were 15,132 people in Boston or 17,561 including Skirbeck and Skirbeck Quarter. That was more than in Lincoln or any other town in Lincolnshire. This increase was not caused by the original townsfolk having more children, but by people attracted here from far distant places. Many of these young men married local women, so very soon there was an increase in the number of babies, though many died young.

The newcomers included those from nearby villages such as lawyer Samuel Tunnard from Frampton, bank clerk Pishey Thompson from Freiston, and John Oldrid from Hagworthingham who went into business as a draper. Others came from adjoining counties, and some from London like Italian-born Dominic Gugeri, a watchmaker who set up in the Market Place. Even as late as the 1830s, William Lewin arrived from London to be engineer and surveyor to the Witham Drainage commissioners; two of his sons set up a timber business that as Harrison and Lewin

lasted until late in the 20th century. One 19th-century business that still survives is Ridlington & Son, the wine and spirit merchants.

The growth of Boston during the Georgian period was due to the increase in traffic through the port. Some of the remaining medieval warehouses were enlarged or rebuilt on the river banks in the town centre, particularly next to Packhouse Quay; more new granaries were built in South Square and behind High Street. Some of these granaries have since been converted for new uses, such as the Sam Newsom Music Centre and the flats in South Square. Grain waggons from Holland Fen came in via West Street and so, about 1800, Bridge Street was created to improve access to the town bridge. A row of shops was built along the north side of the new street, and are still in use today.

As well as new warehouses and granaries, this new traffic needed ships, and therefore sails, rigging, supplies, and sailors. So new businesses were set up close to the river to build ships, make sails and produce ropes and wooden blocks for rigging. Houses were needed for the sailors and workers in the granaries, ships yards, sail lofts and other premises, so there was a need for joiners, bricklayers, slaters, architects and builders. This growing population also meant there were more butchers, bakers, boot and shoemakers, drapers, maltsters and brewers. The existing merchants and ship owners prospered, and others were attracted to join them. Wherever there is money, there will be work for lawyers, so Boston had several of them.

ADVERTISEMENT OF RIDLINGTON & SON 1896
ZZZ04453 (Boston Red Book)

Fact File

Jean Ingelow (1820-97) was born in South Square, the granddaughter of Boston banker William Ingelow, and became a successful poet. Her most famous poem was 'High Tide on the Coast of Lincolnshire'. She was admired here as well as in the United States. Jean might have become Poet Laureate after Alfred Tennyson if Queen Victoria had not thought the job unsuitable for a woman.

The local merchants included Richard Fydell and his son, Thomas, who lived in the house that still bears their name (see page 61). Their extended family dominated the town's political affairs until the 1830s. The first bank in Lincolnshire had been opened in Boston in 1754 by William Garfit and, 20 years later, he took into partnership his great-nephew Bartholomew Claypon. The two families owned the bank until 1891 when it merged with the bank that is now Lloyds TSB. Garfit's Bank moved from High Street to the Market Place in 1864, and the initials of the partners are still over the ground floor windows facing the Market Place.

Newcomers also prospered; by the early 1800s, there were six separate banks owned by local people. Henry Gee was a brewer and merchant who arrived in Boston in 1781 and opened the second Boston bank in 1783 with his local partner, Henry Clark, which traded for nearly 100 years, but was bankrupted in 1874. Their building next to the Town Bridge is now occupied by HSBC.

As more people moved into Boston, more houses were needed. In the early 18th century a few fine houses were built, including Fydell House, 120 High Street, and a new vicarage, but there had been no overall expansion of the town. The real rebuilding of Boston didn't start until the last quarter of the century. Those who had made fortunes in the boom town built grand houses, such as lawyer Tunnard's in Wide Bargate, now Lloyds TSB bank. There was rebuilding in High Street, Wormgate, South End and elsewhere. Many of these were in courts or gardens behind existing houses but were so crowded together that nearly all have since been demolished in slum-clearance programmes. One or two were converted to garages or outhouses in the 20th century but most of those have gone too.

Then from about 1790, for the first time since the Middle Ages, whole new streets were created on green fields around the edges of the old town, and some along roads leading out of town. One of these, Witham Place, still preserves much of its

WIDE BARGATE 2005 B155708k (Neil Wright)

The two houses on the right are the home and office built by Samuel Tunnard, lawyer, c1790. Later occupiers included the Oldrid family in late 19th century.

original appearance. This was part of a new development between Strait Bargate and Witham Town that included Red Lion Street and several other narrower streets behind Witham Place. The new street giving access to this area from Strait Bargate was, with a wonderful lack of imagination, given the name of New Street! Pen Street and other streets were built on fields between Wide Bargate and Main Ridge. The third major area of greenfield development in the early 1800s was around Liquorpond Street and King Street. The controversy in recent years about the divorce of the Prince of Wales is nothing compared to the scandal of King George IV's divorce in the 1820s; it is believed that the names King Street, George Street, Queen Street and Innocent Street reflected the popular opinion that 'King George's Queen is Innocent'. It is even said that there used to be an 'Is Lane' in this area! In the 1960s and 1970s, the character of the Pen Street and Liquorpond Street areas was devastated when John Adams Way was cut through them, so they do not look as attractive now as they would have done when first built.

As the town expanded outwards it crossed the borough boundary into Skirbeck on the east and Skirbeck Quarter on the south. In Skirbeck, the development was mainly along the banks of the Maud Foster Drain, including Horncastle Road, Drainside (now Windsor Bank), and Spilsby Road. The new buildings in Skirbeck Quarter were on the section of London Road facing the river, and included warehouses, pubs and private houses that were part of the port. The area covered by the town just about doubled, but the population in 1851 was about four times that of 1770, so the people were more crowded, and living conditions in some parts became pretty awful.

WINDSOR BANK 2005 B155710k (Neil Wright)

In the early 19th century many terraces were built end-to-end along the east bank of the Maud Foster Drain. They were in Skirbeck parish as the boundary here ran down the middle of the drain.

Dr Taylor of Heckington visited Boston in 1790 to be horrified by the large number of infant deaths. Even by 1790, the population of Boston was about 5,500, nearly double the 3,000 or so of 40 years earlier. The Revd Samuel Partridge, who succeeded Calthrop as Vicar of Boston in 1785, was concerned about the bodily health of his parishioners, and encouraged the formation of a dispensary in 1795 where the poor could have access to a doctor and receive medication; the costs

were covered by charitable donations from the well-to-do. The building used by the dispensary for a number of years was the Church House at the end of Wormgate, opposite the Stump.

The rebuilding of Boston coincided with the invention of the terrace as a form of housing, rows of houses built to look like a grand mansion. The first in Boston was the Corporation Building in the Market Place, built in 1769-72, but others followed in the new residential areas including Drainside, Liquorpond Street (now gone) and elsewhere. One interesting attempt at unofficial town planning is in Pen Street where a house was built exactly opposite the end of Grove Street with two matching cottages like 'pavilions' on either side.

PEN STREET 2005 B155711k (Neil Wright)

An architectural statement in Pen Street, opposite the junction with Grove Street.

Jeptha Pacey was an early 19th century architect who designed a number of churches in the fens north of Boston, and perhaps also the Assembly Rooms, but as a builder and developer he was also responsible for several blocks of slum property around the town. His wife's uncle, John Watson, was another developer (of a different type) during Boston's Georgian prosperity; his buildings included the fine terrace 1-10 Witham Place, and a more modest but respectable terrace in Red Lion Street between Wormgate and Chapel Street. The Witham Place houses were called the Number Slabs because they had been given house numbers by 1803, which was about 60 years earlier than most other properties in the town.

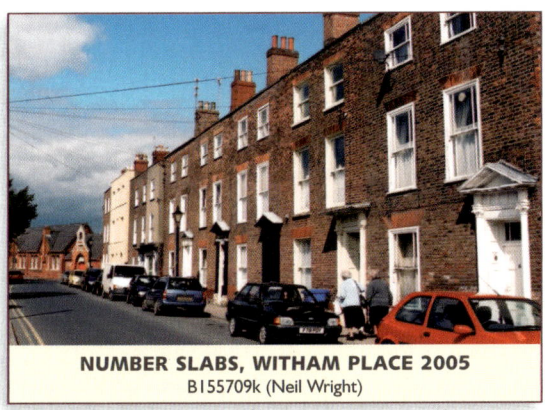
NUMBER SLABS, WITHAM PLACE 2005
B155709k (Neil Wright)

This terrace and other Georgian houses were built on a greenfield site north of the town in the 1790s; the road was then still part of Wormgate, and led towards Witham Town.

THE CORPORATION BUILDING (NOW EXCHANGE BUILDING), MARKET PLACE 2005
B155712k (Neil Wright)

The prosperity of the town is reflected in the rebuilding of the town centre. A series of 17th-century buildings within the Market Place were removed, and then most of the buildings along the west side were swept away in what would now be called 'town centre redevelopment'. New ones were erected including the Corporation Building, Assembly Rooms, and a crescent of six shops from No 45 to Church Lane. The Corporation Building put up in 1769-72 was a mix of public offices and private houses, with the fish market in the centre of the ground floor behind arches that still remain, and a police court on the floor above. The modern Assembly Rooms were built in 1822, though the big bay window was added later. All of these changes have given us the Market Place we see today. A warehouse in the Market Place used as a temporary theatre was replaced in 1806 when a new theatre was built in Red Lion Street. A pleasure park, called Vauxhall Gardens, was created in Skirbeck in 1815, and the road leading to it is still called Vauxhall Road.

THE ASSEMBLY ROOMS, MARKET PLACE 2005
B155713k (Neil Wright)

AN ADVERTISEMENT FOR THE PEACOCK AND ROYAL HOTEL IN THE MARKET PLACE 1896
ZZZ04454 (Boston Red Book)

A regular visitor to Boston in Georgian times was Joseph Banks (1743-1820), the rich and energetic squire of Revesby to the north of the town. Joseph Banks, who inherited his estate and an income of £6,000 a year in 1764 when he was 21, was the clever young gentleman in charge of the

The work of the turnpike trusts in the 18th century meant that roads were good enough for people to start stagecoach services between towns. By the early 1800s Boston had regular services to London and other main towns, and coaching inns like the Peacock in the market place, where Boots is now, prospered greatly. They were also where knowledge and information from London arrived first.

Fact File

In the early 19th century, before people knew better, Boston was a seaside resort! Visitors from inland counties came here, and used bathing huts to swim in the wide tidal river near Skirbeck Church. The Neptune public house behind the sea bank still survives though now it is a private house. A few miles further along the coast is Freiston Shore, overlooking the Wash. It had two hotels, of which the Plummers remains.

THE TOWN HALL AND FYDELL HOUSE 1899 43298

scientific side of Captain Cook's expedition on HMS 'Endeavour' to the South Pacific in 1768-71. When he came back to Britain he became notorious for having enjoyed the uninhibited Tahitian women! He also became a figure of national importance in court and scientific circles, becoming President of the Royal Society, a friend of King George III, a knight, and involved in anything important that happened in Lincolnshire. He often visited Mr Fydell's house in Boston, and there is still a fine portrait of Sir Joseph Banks in the guildhall next door.

For many years Sir Joseph helped other people to follow scientific exploration, and it was due to him that many Lincolnshire men were involved in the exploration of Australia, including George Bass, surgeon of Boston, Matthew Flinders of Donington and John Franklin of Spilsby. In the late 1700s, Bass (after whom the Bass Strait is named) had been apprenticed to Mr Francis who had premises in Strait Bargate, probably on part of the site now covered by Oldrids. His mother had run the Rope and Anchor Inn in Skirbeck Quarter (rebuilt in 1803 as the Crown and Anchor) and now 10 London Road (see below). In 1801-02 Flinders mapped the southern coast of Australia and named many places on the Eyre Peninsula from Lincolnshire: Port Lincoln; Boston Island; Revesby Cove; Cape Donington; and others. Before sailing on his ill-fated voyage to the Arctic in 1842, Sir John Franklin visited some of his Lincolnshire relatives; it is believed that one of the last houses he stayed in was 120 High Street, now called Franklin Lodge.

Boston was growing commercially, but improvements in the quality of life only occurred when they served commerce. The pilot service was organised in 1774 and, in 1776, an Act of Parliament set up a body of men as 'Lighting and Watching Commissioners'

LONDON ROAD, SKIRBECK QUARTER 2005 B155714k (Neil Wright)

The tall building in the centre is 10 London Road, which was the Crown and Anchor until the late 19th century when the licence was moved to smaller premises (since demolished) six doors to the left.

DOUGHTY QUAY 1890 26066t

to provide street lighting and a basic police service by night-watchmen. An Act of 1792 set up 'Improvement Commissioners' to look after the streets of the town, paving and cleaning them, removing encroachments, widening them where necessary, and also creating new ones like Bridge Street and New Street.

Under an Act of 1812, the harbour commissioners improved the port by removing some wharves and building new river walls; these brick walls topped by stone can still be seen on the east bank from the Assembly Rooms to the Sam Newsom Music Centre, and on the bank opposite. New public warehouses were built on Packhouse Quay (in South Street) and Doughty Quay (in High Street). The latter still survives as a

private house. These river works were carried out under a scheme designed by the engineer John Rennie, who had already drained the East, West and Wildmore Fens and designed a new town bridge, which remained until 1913. The fen drainage works included widening Maud Foster drain, building a new sluice at its southern end, and erecting three cast-iron footbridges of which Hospital Bridge and one at Cowbridge are still in use. Other improvements in the Georgian period included a gas works to provide gas lighting for the town in 1826. A proper water supply was provided by a company in 1848, with a reservoir at Miningsby next to Revesby on the edge of the Wolds, and piped from there into the town.

Boston had changed because of commerce but the Grammar School had not. Other schools were provided to meet the town's needs. Two charity schools - the Blue Coat School and Laughton's School - had opened in the early 18th century. In 1815 two larger schools were opened, the British (Anglican) School and the National (Non-conformist) School. In addition, there were a number of small schools or 'academies' held in private houses. The Grammar School was failing, and for a number of years in the 1840s it actually closed. It reopened in October 1847 but its real revival only started in 1850 after a new headmaster was appointed.

Boston was not only the largest town and the commercial capital of Lincolnshire in the early 19th century but was also the first town in the county to industrialise. There were brewers and tanners as well as shipbuilders, sailmakers, rope makers, coachbuilders and saddlers. One coachbuilder was John Mumford who had left the town but returned in 1834 and set up in business in West Street. He lapsed into drink and moved to Brixton in London in 1844, leaving his Boston business premises in the hands of his mortgagee. His daughter Catherine had seen at first hand the evils of drink in the streets of Boston and, after marrying William Booth in 1855, she and her husband became the founders of what is now the Salvation Army.

THE MARKET PLACE AND THE CHURCH 1890 26068

This photograph shows the gas 'Five Lamps' in the middle of the Market Place. The first lamp was erected in 1842 and four others added in 1847. They were replaced by electric lights in 1925, but were still called the 'Five Lamps', and later moved to Liquorpond Street.

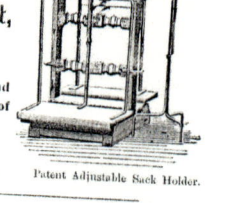

PURE WATER—HEALTH !!!

GEORGE CHEAVIN'S IMPROVED PATENT GOLD MEDAL SELF-CLEANSING RAPID WATER FILTER.

The only Filter which effectually removes Lead, Lime, Iron, Sewage, Organic and Mineral Matter, and excels all others in Mechanical and Chemical Action, and is the most effective means known of Purifying Water for domestic, manufacturing and general purposes.

Can be thoroughly Cleaned by any one in a few minutes, and retain its Purifying Power for 20 years.

Appointment by Special Warrants, Filter Manufacturer, to HER MAJESTY THE QUEEN, H.R.H. PRINCE of WALES, The EMPEROR NAPOLEON III., The British Government, &c. Awarded Six Gold and Silver Medals, in addition to 45 First-Class Prizes from the leading Exhibitions of England and the Continent.

6200 Physicians, Surgeons and Chemists have these Filters in use, (and strongly recommend them to every Householder.)

Copy of *unsolicited Testimonial.*
Marlborough House, Pall Mall, S.W., Oct. 13th, 1871.
Sir,—Sir Wm. Knolleys desires me to inform you that the Filter you supplied to H. R. H. the Prince of Wales gives great satisfaction. I am, Sir, your obedient Servant,
Mr. G. CHEAVIN. WILLIAM PEEL.

1200 References and Testimonials in its favour from those who have used it and tested its merits, including names of the highest standing in the Medical and Scientific world, on application. Price List Free.

G. CHEAVIN, PATENTEE & SOLE MANUFACTURER, BOSTON, LINCOLNSHIRE.

N.B.—Merchants, Factors, Wholesale and Retail Ironmongers, Implement Agents, and others, who can Sell my Filter, abroad or in this country, will receive my best attention; and will find, in consequence of the popularity and important advantages of my Filter, it will meet with an easy and profitable sale.

Works: Mill Lane.
By His Majesty's Royal Letters Patent, No. 9601.

W. S. BARRETT,

Wireworker, Weighing Machine & Potato Riddle Maker,

106 & 108 West Street,

BOSTON.

Contractor for the Repairs and Maintenance of all kinds of Weighing Apparatus.

Estimates on Application.

Patent Adjustable Sack Holder.

W.S.B. begs to call attention to his **Patent Potato Riddle** and **Patent Sack Holder** for Weighing Machines, both of which are found to have many advantages over the old kinds, and is prepared to supply same wholesale and retail.

WORKING PEOPLE FURNISH your HOUSES at SCHRIMSHAW'S.

THE CHEAPEST HOUSE

POLISHED CHAIRS, half-dozen 10/- to 21/-. High back ARM CHAIRS, unpolished, 5/- and 5/6. Polished Lath Back Chairs, from 4/6. Flock Lath Back Rocker, polished. Flock Mattress 6/8, Bass, full size, from 12/6. Flock Mattress 6/8, 12/6 to 17/6. Feather Beds, 30/ to 50/-. Spring Mattresses, from 17/6. Straw Mattresses, full size, 6/6 to 9/-. Bolstead, full size from 11/9. Brass Rail Bedsteads full size 16/6, 10/6. Do. do. in Mahogany Frames, 20/-. Gent's Easy Chairs (in Hair), 24/- to 35/-. Ladies' Easy Chair, mahogany, 21/-. American Leather Couches 20/- to 30/-. Mahogany Couches, Home-made, from 42/-. Spring Seated, in Hair, 42/6, 57/6 and 65/-. Home-made Polished Deal Drawers from 20/-. THE BEST VALUE (18/) BOSTON Mahogany Drawers, Home-made 40/- to 65/-. Deal Pembroke Tables from 6/9, 8/6, and 10/6. Mahogany Polished Tables from 22/-, 45/- to 50/-. Mahogany or Walnut Chefonieres, 45/-, 50/-. Marble Wash stands in Glass Back 35/-. Marble Wash stands in Mahogany or Birch from 11/6. Looking Glasses, from 6/1 to 70/-. Kitchen Fenders, 2/6. Room Fenders, 1/- to 7/6. Fire Irons from 3/6 to 16/-. A large stock of Tin Boxes from 4/6 1/9, 2/-, 2/6, 3/-, 4/6, 5/-, 6/9, 7/6, 8/6, 9/6, 10/6. Wood Boxes from 5/6 to 15/-. Perambulators from 21/6 up to 42/4/-. Washing Machine from 70/-. Wringer Machine, warranted, from 27/6. Lock stitch Sewing Machine from 30/- with polished cover, £2/12/6.

THE LARGEST STOCK OF HOME MADE FURNITURE IN BOSTON TO SELECT FROM

SCHRIMSHAW'S FURNITURE WORK SHOPS

A HOUSE FURNISHED FROM £5 TO £50

SALE & SHOW ROOMS

FLOORING DEPARTMENT

OUR MOTTO — SMALL PROFITS & QUICK RETURNS

SCHRIMSHAW 24 DOLPHIN LANE BOSTON

IN BOSTON.

TUXFORD INVENTED STEAM THRASHING SETS

A STEAM THRASHING SET ZZZ04458 ('Lincolnshire Towns and Industry 1700-1914' by N R Wright, 1982)

The idea of having a moveable steam engine to power a moveable thrashing machine was thought of by the Boston engineering firm of Tuxford and Sons in 1842. Until about 50 years ago, country roads in Britain and other parts of the world were filled at harvest time by steam thrashing sets going from farm to farm to thrash the corn and separate the wheat from the chaff. Each 'Set' comprised a steam traction engine, a thrashing machine, an elevator, and a hut for the workmen to live in as they moved about. From the 1880s to the 1950s many such sets were made by several English engineering firms until combine harvesters replaced them.

In 1803 William Howden started an iron foundry in Witham Town, and in 1839 produced the first portable steam engine made in Lincolnshire. A few years later William Wedd Tuxford started an engineering works around his corn mill at Mount Bridge; this became the Boston and Skirbeck Iron Works when his sons joined his business in about 1840. Tuxford's office block still survives, now partly occupied by a hairdresser. Tuxford's engines sold worldwide and, though the firm closed in 1885, you can still see early Tuxford engines in museums in Paris and Sweden.

A local bank clerk called Pishey Thompson recognised that he was seeing momentous changes in the life of the town, and made a point of interviewing older inhabitants, looking through old records, and collecting statistics on the changes he was seeing. When he emigrated to the United States in 1819, he published the information he had already got and, on returning to England in 1846, he spent his retirement working on an updated version of his book which was published ten years later. Maybe it was due to Pishey Thompson's contacts with both Bostons that American money helped to restore a chapel in the Stump in memory of John Cotton, and that a short-lived adult education establishment in our town, founded in 1851, was called the Boston Athenaeum after its more illustrious predecessor in Massachusetts.

In the early 19th century there about a dozen windmills in Boston producing flour, and many were on sites that had been used for centuries. The only one remaining is the Maud Foster Mill built in 1819 for the brothers Thomas and Isaac Reckitt from Wainfleet, and later operated by the Ostler family. It ceased working in 1949, was restored as a landmark in 1953, and since 1987 has been brought back to work by the Waterfield family.

OSTLER'S MILL c1950 B155015

The house in the centre is 7 South End, where Miss Leonora Thompson lived from the 1830s to 1861. Her brother Pishey Thompson wrote some of his history of the town in the 'little back room, upstairs' in the 1850s.

THE FERRY 1899 43303

The picture painted so far of Georgian Boston is pretty positive, but there was a darker side. Boston nowadays might seem rowdy when there is a home football match or when the pubs close on a Saturday night, but in the 1830s the members of the Corporation were so worried about the possibility of serious rioting that they called for help from the government, and troops were sent into the town. That achieved the desired result, but not everyone was happy about the town being occupied as the following report in The Stamford Mercury newspaper in January 1832 shows: 'A number of corn-porters and boatmen employed near Bargate bridge, Boston, have been in the habit of repeatedly abusing the Dragoons when they go out on parade. On Wednesday morning [25 January] one fellow threw a potatoe at the soldiers, which struck the Serjeant-major. He promptly caused the cowardly ruffian to be taken before the Magistrates, who ordered him to pay a fine of a sovereign and the costs.' (A sovereign was a £1 coin - a lot of money in those days.)

Why were things so bad that troops had to be called in? It was because the bloody French Revolution (started in 1789) had so horrified the ruling classes in Britain that for 40 years they resisted all efforts to reform national and local government. In Boston, as elsewhere, the Corporation was self-elected, and they would not appoint anyone onto the council who disagreed with them. Many of Boston's rich new businessmen were excluded from the running of the town, even when they politely asked to be appointed. William Tuxford and some other reformers were radical (the pub next to his works is still named the Napoleon after the revolutionary hero), but most reformers were moderate Whigs. The only difference between them and members of the Corporation was that the newcomers were Nonconformists, not Anglicans. They were Baptists and Unitarians, and after 1800 there were increasing numbers of Methodists.

It was the Fydell family and their wider clan of relations who ran Boston and kept a tight control on affairs. Richard and his son, Thomas, were MPs for the town as well as being mayors on several occasions. The clan included the husbands of Fydell daughters and nieces, such as John Betts, Edward Wilford and Augustus Duggan who were all merchants, and Henry Rogers the town clerk and family solicitor to the Fydells. Even after Thomas died in 1812 and his son became a country gentleman in Rutland, the wider Fydell clan continued to control the town until the great reforms of the 1830s gave the ratepayers the right to elect the councillors.

In December 1835 the members of Boston Corporation were democratically elected for the first time, and the reformers swept the board - not a single member of the old Corporation was elected. The first mayor of the reformed Corporation was John Rawson, a draper and local director of the Stamford, Spalding and Boston Bank who lived at

THE STAMFORD, SPALDING AND BOSTON BANK 1899 43293x

The new premises of the Stamford, Spalding and Boston Bank (now Barclays Bank), erected in 1875-6 at 52 Market Place.

Skirbeck House, in a lane (off Horncastle Road) now called Rawson's Lane after him. One of the first actions of the reformers was to sell off all the gold and silver plate that had been used for the feasts and celebrations of the old Corporation. Other reforms transferred the guildhall to charity trustees (its use by the council gradually declined), and also modernised the poor law that led to the building of a great Union Workhouse in Skirbeck Road, of which the entrance block still remains.

THE SURVIVING SECTION OF THE FORMER UNION WORKHOUSE, SKIRBECK ROAD 2005 B155715k (Neil Wright)

THE SESSIONS HOUSE 1893 32072

This was built in 1848 for some of the courts previously held in the guildhall.

THE INTERIOR OF ST BOTOLPH'S CHURCH 1893 32069

This shows the church ceiling and new pews for 2,000 people after the restoration of the 1850s.

SIR GEORGE GILBERT SCOTT (1811-78)

This eminent Victorian architect had several jobs in the Boston area, including the Union Workhouse (1837), restoration of St Botolph's Church (started 1845), and Cotton Chapel (started 1857), Holy Trinity Church, Spilsby Road (1846-48) and restoration of St Nicholas's Church, Skirbeck (1869-75). He married his cousin, Caroline Oldrid, whose father had the draper's business in Strait Bargate. A number of their sons followed the same profession, and a later member of the family was responsible for the iconic red telephone box, the Anglican cathedral in Liverpool and the Thames-side power station that is now the Tate Modern.

A VICTORIAN ROMANCE

Boston Town Clerk Buxton Kenrick resigned in 1856 after 24 years in office and went to France. He became a partner in a silk factory that became bankrupt in 1861, and then he moved to Italy where, in his 60s, he joined Garibaldi's forces fighting for the unification of Italy. He also started a passionate affair with 28-year-old Miss Gray. His wife's relations stopped sending him funds, and 62-year-old Kenrick and his young lover made a suicide pact, filling each other's clothes with sand, lying down at the water's edge and drowning in the Bay of Naples.

In the 1840s Boston was a rich, flourishing town; but then came the railways. The first lines were opened in October 1848, from Boston to London, Grimsby and Lincoln. The first winter showed what was going to happen. Severe weather stopped all shipping in and out of the port, but the railway kept going and handled all traffic to and from London. The shipping of the port was quickly much reduced, ships were laid up, and granaries in the port were replaced by new facilities next to the railway. The port's prosperity evaporated. A later railway was opened westwards to Sleaford and Grantham but it failed to save the port as ships were now larger and needed a wet dock, so that they did not have to sit on the mud at low tide. As the new railway was built alongside a straight road for eight miles across Holland Fen, the railway company had to build a tall fence of wooden boards to separate the railway and road - the boards have now gone, but the road is still known as the Boardsides Road.

The Great Northern Railway ran two-thirds of all the railway lines in Lincolnshire and Boston was the centre of their activity in the county. Until the GNR developed the Plant at Doncaster, its engineering department, responsible for designing locomotives, carriages, and other rolling stock, was located in Boston at

This is the original entrance, restored from 1991-93.

THE RAILWAY STATION, WEST STREET 2005   B155716k (Neil Wright)

The original timber railway bridge over the Witham, built
in 1848, was replaced by the present bridge in 1885.

WITHAM BANK AND THE BOSTON STUMP c1955   B155035

Broadfield Lane - the last buildings there were only demolished in the opening years of the 21st century. But the railway also employed people not only in its passenger station and goods station, but also in a sacking store (which still stands), a creosote works (where wooden railway sleepers were treated with preservative), a civil engineers' yard (to maintain its buildings and track) and, later, a plant that produced gas to light railway carriages. By 1912 the GNR was the largest employer in Boston, and a great many of its workers lived in the streets next to the railway line through the town. Nowadays only the passenger station and a signal box are in use by the railway, but the sacking store, goods warehouse and civil engineers' buildings have all found new uses.

The opening of the railway in 1848 turned West Street into one of the town's main shopping streets, and new premises included The Boston Guardian works of 1887. The number of new jobs on the railway was smaller than those lost in the port and related functions, so the town suffered and, in 1881, the population was no greater than it had been in 1851! For 30 years Boston was again in the doldrums. It lost its vitality. One of the few public improvements during this period was the new cemetery on Horncastle Road, opened in 1856.

THE CEMETERY 1899 43306

94, WEST STREET, BOSTON.

AN ADVERTISEMENT FOR THE BOSTON GUARDIAN WORKS 1896 ZZZ04459 (Boston Red Book)

Several proposals were put forward to create a company that would build a wet dock at Boston, but private enterprise failed to achieve it. Boston Dock only came into being when the Corporation worked with the river

THE BATH GARDENS 1893 32075

Part of the riverside path, much overgrown, still survives in 2005 south of the old swimming baths, but the reservoir has been filled in.

and drainage authorities to widen and deepen the river, create a new cut over two miles long through shifting sands into the Wash, and build the dock at public expense. And that was the saving of the port. The area where the dock was built was still fields until that date, and two windmills on the river bank had to be demolished. The main people to propose the scheme were John Cabourn Simonds and his son, William Turner Simonds, who had two large seed-crushing mills in the town (the Britannia Mill at the corner of South Street and Spayne Lane has been converted to flats). The dock was to be the basis of the town's re-growth in the 20th century.

THE PEOPLE'S PARK AND THE HOSPITAL 1899 43309

This is part of the People's Park next to the General Hospital; Victorian developments that are both now gone.

THE PEOPLE'S PARK AND THE HOSPITAL 1899   43309

CHAPTER FOUR

20TH-CENTURY
BOSTON

A DOMINANT FACTOR in the life of Boston in the 20th century was Boston Dock. It attracted both of the author's grandfathers to the town! James Ainsworth was a master mariner like his father before him, and James Wright came here to work for the Great Northern Railway which itself expanded to meet the needs of the dock. In many ways, for Boston the 20th century started on 15th December 1884 when the first ship entered the dock. Boston Dock prospered throughout the 20th century and, for most of that time, was owned by Boston Corporation. In its early years it developed into a substantial fishing port with two deep-sea fishing companies, a fish quay and ice-house, and ship repairing facilities. Cargo ships no longer went upriver into the old port in the town centre; that was only used as moorings for fishing smacks.

The Market Place on Wednesdays and Saturdays is still the throbbing heart of Boston. The architecture is an interesting mix, with a few tall Victorian buildings mingling with their Georgian neighbours.

MARKET PLACE 1899 43297

THE DOCKS 1899 43305

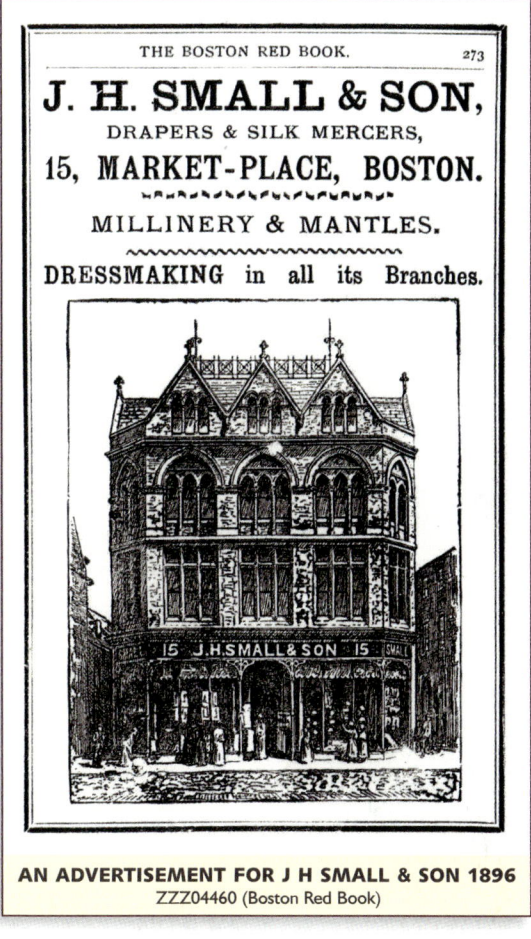

AN ADVERTISEMENT FOR J H SMALL & SON 1896
ZZZ04460 (Boston Red Book)

The most extravagant Victorian building in the Market Place was Small's drapers shop at the corner of Dolphin Lane.

The dock was created by public authorities after private enterprise had attempted and failed. During the 20th century central and local government, and a range of other publicly funded agencies, provided a wider range of services than governments had ever done before, and this century may be remembered as the golden age of public service. In Boston, a key event was the opening of the municipal buildings in West Street on 16 June 1904 by Mayor Joseph Cooke. The building contained the town's fire station, police station with exercise yard, police court, public library and School of Art as well as the council chamber, mayor's parlour, and a few rooms for the town clerk, treasurer and other officers. The council also provided the assembly rooms, swimming baths and people's park, and in 1904 they were given back the guildhall which timber merchant Frank Harrison had bought from the charity trustees.

But the Corporation did not provide all the services in the town, and in Skirbeck and Skirbeck Quarter it provided no services at all - those suburbs were part of Boston Rural District (formed 1894) until the 1930s when the town took them over. Other services were provided by Holland County Council (formed 1888), the Board of Guardians and the school boards. The County Council built its own headquarters in 1927, and this is now Boston Library operated by Lincolnshire County Council. Within the town the Corporation also had its own police force, but Skirbeck and Skirbeck Quarter were served by the Lincolnshire constabulary who had their own police station, later a co-op store next to the Black Sluice. During the course of the century more powers were given to the Corporation, Rural District Council and County Council as the School Boards and Board of Guardians were abolished, in 1902 and 1929 respectively, and other new services were introduced.

THE RIVER c1955 B155067

COUNTY HALL, CHURCH CLOSE 2005 B155717k (Neil Wright)

This was the headquarters of Holland County Council from 1927 to 1974. The building now houses Boston Library and the Registration Service of Lincolnshire County Council.

The national government also developed local offices. A central post office had been built in High Street in 1882-85, but in 1907 it was replaced by the present building in Wide Bargate which was soon extended to include the sorting office and the telephone exchange, where the author's mother worked for a while. Later public buildings included the employment exchange in West Street, built in 1939 in place of rented accommodation, and later the tax office in Norfolk Street, with hutments out in the back including the driver testing office.

Boston did not have a public supply of electricity until 1926, about 40 years after it had been available in London and elsewhere. Until then Boston Dock and some large factories had to produce their own electricity. The gas 'Five Lamps' in the Market Place was replaced by an electronic lamp standard (with just two lamps!) and 50 years later that was moved to its present site in Liquorpond Street.

In the period from 1851 to 1881 there had been no increase in the town's population, and after the dock was opened many newcomers could move into the stock of existing houses. From the 1890s several new streets of middle-class houses were built on remaining greenfield sites within the town and some even further out. One site on the north side

THE 'FIVE LAMPS' IN THE MARKET PLACE c1965
B155103x

TOWER STREET 1893 32065

of Bargate developed from 1894 onwards, and became Tunnard Street, Thorold Street and Tawney Street with a large part preserved as an open space that in the 1930s became the Central Park. The area between Main Ridge and Skirbeck Road, to the west of the Barditch, was not released by the heirs of the Fydell family for development until the late 1930s; that was held up by the Second World War, and the author can still remember corn being harvested on the east side of York Street in the 1950s. Plans to demolish Fydell House to provide access to this land led to the formation of the Boston Preservation Trust in 1935, and access was gained instead through the farmyard, which is now part of Rowley Road. One of the pictures in this book shows a distant view of haystacks in the farmyard (page 88-89). Other housing filled the areas between Carlton Road and Brothertoft Road and spread out in ribbons along roads leading out of town: Sleaford Road, Spilsby Road, Tower Road, London Road and Eastfield Road. By the 1930s, nearly a quarter of the population lived in Skirbeck and Skirbeck Quarter, which were in Boston rural district. They had different education, housing and police authorities, and it was not until 1932 that the boundaries of Boston were expanded to include all of Skirbeck Quarter and the built-up parts of Skirbeck.

THE HUSSEY TOWER 1893 32076

To the right of the Tower you can make out haystacks in the farmyard (now the top end of Rowley Road) and behind the Grammar School. The fields attached to that farm are now Rowley Road, Pilgrim Road, York Street, the Grammar School playing fields and Boston College.

THE DOCKS 1890   26082

In earlier times, war had only affected the soldiers and sailors directly involved and people who happened to live on or near the battlefield, or the route of the marching army. But in the 20th century the concept of 'total war' meant that everyone could be involved, and this affected Boston as much as elsewhere. The First World War started in August 1914 and, between the 22nd and 26th of that month, the German navy sank 26 British trawlers in the North Sea, ten from Boston and fourteen from Grimsby. Fishermen were taken prisoner and those of neutral nationality were soon released, but the British fishermen were sent to prison camps including 88 from Boston. Later in the war, more Boston fishing boats were

PRISONERS OF WAR

During the First World War (1914-18) Britain and Germany agreed to exchange prisoners of war who were incapable of military service. In December 1917, neutral Dutch ships brought disabled soldiers and civilians to Boston Deeps where they were transferred to tugs that brought them into Boston Dock. The Fish Pontoon on the dock had been made into a reception area with rest rooms, etc, and from there the soldiers were loaded onto hospital trains that took them to London and Nottingham. The prisoners included some Boston fishermen who had been captured in the North Sea; altogether over 5,000 prisoners landed at Boston. German prisoners were taken back in return.

sunk with the loss of many lives. The first two Boston fishermen to be repatriated because of age got home in November 1917, and another sixteen returned in January 1918. The rest of the survivors did not get home until after the end of the war in November 1918.

On a happy day in August 1916 Alice Oldrid, one of four sisters who then owned the famous drapers shop in Boston, married Alan James Derrick of Redcar on Teesside, a 2nd Lieutenant in the 7th Reserve Batallion of the Northumberland Fusiliers. She was the envy of her sisters Edith, Mabel and Dorothy who were still unmarried. But her joy lasted less than three months. On 16 November 1916, her husband was officially reported as missing and she became a widow. Alice never remarried, and her three sisters stayed spinsters living for many years in Greyfriars next to the Grammar School. Over 9,000 Boston men fought in the First World War and deaths amounted to 943 men and two women. In the Second World War Boston suffered little damage, partly because it was flown over by bombers on their way to inland targets using the Stump as a landmark, and only if they had some bombs left on their way home might they be dropped on Boston. In the Second World War there were 325 people from Boston who died in military service.

THE WAR MEMORIAL, WIDE BARGATE 2005 B155718k (Neil Wright)

THE WESLEYAN CHURCH 1893 32074

The Centenary Methodist Church, shown here, was burnt down in 1909 and the present church on the site was opened in 1911.

The direct involvement of the civilian population in the horrors of war might be one of the factors contributing to the decline of religious belief and worship during the 20th century. When the Centenary Methodist Chapel was destroyed by fire on 24 June 1909, the congregation responded magnificently and the new chapel on the site was re-opened in 1911, and is still in use. However since then many churches and chapels have closed in Boston, including the Anglican St James's and St Aiden's, the large Trinity Street Methodist Chapel, the Congregational Church in Grove Street and two Baptist Churches in Liquorpond Street. Those that remained had much smaller congregations at the end of the century compared with 100 years earlier. The author's grandfather, like many railwaymen, attended the Primitive Methodist Chapel in West Street, and eventually became one of its trustees but, since his death in 1968, the family are lapsed Methodists. Many families have had a similar experience.

Agriculture had entered a period of decline at the end of the 19th century, and Lincolnshire farmers diversified, turning this area into one of the main suppliers of seeds and vegetables for the whole country. At first the produce was mainly moved long distance by train, horse wagons and then motor trucks bringing it from the farm to the station. After the First World War fleets of motor vehicles were developed to do the whole journey, and goods services on the railways went into steady decline.

Fact File

Boston used to be a centre of the feather industry, and Fogarty's still exists. Geese were bred on the Lincolnshire fens in great numbers and their feathers were plucked twice a year to fill feather beds and pillows. In the 19th century there were several factories in Boston to purify the feathers. One built by Mrs F S Anderson & Co near the railway station in 1877 has a great white swan on top of the factory; it is now apartments.

Feathers

EVERY DESCRIPTION OF BED FEATHERS PURCHASED FOR IMMEDIATE CASH . . .

Write for Prices before calling elsewhere
Banker's Reference—National Provincial Bank Limited

E. FOGARTY & CO.
LIMITED
Down & Feather Purifiers

TRINITY STREET, BOSTON, LINCS
Telephone 217

AN ADVERTISEMENT FOR E FOGARTY & CO LTD
1935 ZZZ04461 (Kelly's Boston Directory)

Mobile sales offices like these were in use by corn merchants and seed merchants from the late 19th century to the 1960s, pulled in by horse each market day from the Corporation yard at the end of Sibsey Lane. They lined the pavement from Cornhill Lane to Craythorne Lane.

MARKET PLACE 1899 43295

This changing agriculture also led to old granaries in the town centre being converted to other uses. Some were taken over by seed merchants and others by firms who installed machinery to dry locally grown peas. This was in the days before frozen peas, and the dried peas were sold by the sackfull. The dried pea industry had only a limited life. Johnson's Seeds became the largest privately owned seed firm in the country, with two large seed stores in London Road, but it failed at the end of the century, and its buildings have been demolished. For several years in the middle of the century there were two firms producing tinned fruit and vegetables in Boston - Lin Can near the Black Sluice, and United Canners in Norfolk Street. However, two important long established firms still continue - Fogarty's, which has now moved from its old sites in Trinity Street and Mount Bridge to Fishtoft Road, and Magnadata in Norfolk Street (part of Norcross) which is the direct successor of Fisher Clark's international label business.

Fact File

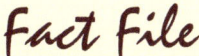

When the Romans invaded this country, the ancient Britons painted themselves with woad. This natural blue dye continued in use until the 20th century when chemical dyes replaced it. There were a number of farms producing woad in the Boston area, and also the mills to process it. They were at Brothertoft in the 1830s, Witham Town in the 1840s, and near Skirbeck Church until the early 20th century. That last business gave its name to the Woad Farm council housing estate. Woad was an anti-social product, the workers getting hands stained blue that couldn't be removed, and producing an awful stink that filled their houses.

Boston ceased to be a significant fishing port in 1922 when a dispute led Fred Parkes, owner of the Boston Deep Sea Fishing Company, to remove his fleet to Fleetwood in Lancashire. The dispute arose after the SS 'Lockwood' went aground in the channel leading from

Boston Dock to the sea and was stuck there for several months. Fred Parkes organised the removal of the 'Lockwood' but the Corporation disputed his bill, and that was the last straw in determining him to remove his operations from the town. Since the Boston Deep Sea Fishing Company left, inshore fishing has continued with small smacks that are tied up in the river, and do not use the dock.

A major change to the physical appearance of Boston in the 20th century was the number of council houses built by the Corporation and Boston Rural District Council. The RDC had built its first council houses in 1914, 44 spread over eight parishes, and the Corporation built its first houses in 1926 in Westfield Avenue followed by more in Sherwood Avenue in 1928. In the late 1930s, several new streets of council houses were built in the Carlton Road/Fenside Road area and the streets were named after people from Boston's past including Cotton, Laughton, Taverner and Ingram. Then in the 1950s/60s another large new estate was laid out on the east side of the town, with Woad Farm Road and Wellington Road as the main spine roads. Other street names on this estate reflected the town's links with Massachusetts - Mayflower, Arbella, Brewster, Winslow, Dudley and Leverett. By 1974 both authorities had over 5,000 council houses but 30 years later they had been transferred to a separate trust.

When the Corporation and Holland County Council became education authorities in 1902 they expanded provision but did not go in for any major rebuilding as the Board Schools were still only six years old. The only

building to be replaced in the early years was the Laughton/Blue Coat School, whose premises in Witham Place were used from 1909 as classes for pupil teachers, and also evening classes. A high school for girls was established in Allan House, Carlton Road, in 1921 with hutments in the grounds, and it moved to new buildings in Spilsby Road in 1939. Under the 1944 Education Act, two secondary modern schools were established in temporary buildings until new buildings were opened for both in 1952. Both schools were named after Alderman Tom Kitwood, former chairman of the education committee. The boys were in Mill Road not far from Skirbeck Church, and the girls were in Robin Hood's Walk; the authorities wanted to keep the sexes well apart! The Grammar School and High School also became secondary schools, and the other schools in the town became primary schools, taking pupils up to the age of eleven. In the second half of the 20th century, all the Board School and Church School buildings were replaced, and the two secondary modern schools have been amalgamated as the Haven High Technology College on the Kitwood Girls' School site. Boston College was opened in 1964, and has expanded in the last 40 years. Residential accommodation and conference facilities were built in the 1990s on the College's Skirbeck Road site to the south of the original buildings.

During the Second World War there was a naval presence in Boston Dock, and they took over the former Union Workhouse as their base, officially known as HMS 'Arbella' to reflect the history of the town. The author's grandfather, James Wright, was in charge of railway operations on the dock during the war, and received a commendation for his diligence. After the navy left, the Union Workhouse was renamed St Johns, and was used for various purposes by Holland County Council, including the offices of the Welfare Department where the author started work in 1962. Eventually the buildings at St Johns were demolished, and most of the site sold for the erection of huge grain silos; but the front block was preserved and, in the closing years of the century, was restored and adapted as a centre for social services.

The centre of Boston also changed during the 20th century, not so much in the buildings as in their occupiers and in the road spaces. Instead of lots of locally owned shops, run by owners who lived above the premises, we now have larger shops that are branches of national chains, often identical in appearance to their branches in other towns. The main exception is Oldrids department store in Strait Bargate,

which the four Oldrid sisters sold in 1918 to the Isaac family who still run it. It rose to become one of the most successful businesses in Lincolnshire, with its Downtown stores as branches. In the 1960s, there were sixteen local shops in Boston selling radios and televisions but now most have gone. The exception is one local business that has a number of branches, Yates and Greenhough, whose proprietors were apprentices to the author's father, Cyril Wright, at Wain and Sharp Ltd in Wormgate. In the Market Place, almost the only new buildings are Marks and Spencer and Boots the chemists at opposite ends. In recent years, new buildings such as MacDonalds and Times Past have had to be faithful copies of the Georgian buildings they replace. As the town grew in the 19th century, local shops were established on street corners in the residential areas, but during the 20th century their business declined and most corner shops have closed or changed to other uses.

This shows the small amount traffic then.

MARKET PLACE c1950 B155005

MARKET PLACE c1955 B155044

BARGATE c1955 B155025

The other unattractive change during the 20th century is that the big open spaces - Market Place, South Square, Wide Bargate, West Street - have become car parks for much of the time. Through traffic has been diverted to the John Adams Way, which was built as an Inner Relief Road in the 1970s following the opening of Haven Bridge in 1966. Several streets in the Pen Street and Liquorpond Street areas have been devastated by the inner relief road. The benefit that did flow from John Adams Way was the removal of through traffic from the Market Place and High Street, and the pedestrianisation of Strait Bargate.

Car ownership meant that people did not need to live within walking distance of work and shops, so new housing estates of detached and semi-detached houses spread in a wide circle around the historic town centre. Ribbon development along the main roads was followed by new estates built to fill the spaces behind the ribbons, development reaching out to Burton Corner on the east and Wyberton on the south and west. Some areas of small houses in the town centre such as Fountain Lane, Silver Street and the Lincoln Lane area, were swept away to leave space for more car parks and new offices or shops. The later creation of Spalding Road along the old railway line, going south from Liqourpond Street, has transformed the character of the south-west part of the town, and has given the chance for the High Street to return to a more peaceful and prosperous life.

Another consequence of increasing car ownership was to move other facilities out to the new edges of Boston. The first and greatest example was the creation of Pilgrim Hospital on the extreme north-east corner of the town in Sibsey Road in 1968. New retail premises, too big to be called shops, were created in Wyberton West for Downtown and Tesco, and houses and industrial buildings were demolished close to the Black Sluice to make way for a Somerfield supermarket and lots of parking space. Playing fields and indoor sports facilities were created between Sleaford Road and the North Forty Foot Drain but, once again, most people needed cars in order to reach them.

The fishing fleet has left but other dock traffic has increased over the years. Timber had been imported from the Baltic for centuries, and the small 19th-century timber yards next to Packhouse Quay and Doughty Quay were replaced by larger yards next to the dock, in Skirbeck Road and over the People's Park. In recent years, these have been replaced by even larger ones extending alongside the Haven downstream from the dock. Other industrial and commercial businesses developed in the Marsh Lane area, some taking advantage of its proximity to the river. Road transport took over from the railway to handle the inland transit of goods, and also served the agricultural and horticultural industries. The dock was sold into private ownership in January 1990 and one consequence was that public access onto the estate was ended - no longer could boys wander over the dock to look at the ships and watch what was happening, as the author had done in his youth.

In the 1970s and 1980s Boston experienced difficulties as seed warehouses and canning factories closed, and local government reorganisation led to Holland County Council being replaced by Lincolnshire County Council in 1974, with its headquarters in Lincoln. Boston Corporation and Boston Rural District were replaced by the new Boston Borough Council. County Hall still houses some county council services, most notably Boston Library and the registration service. The Lincolnshire Standard newspaper used to be printed weekly at its headquarters in Wide Bargate but that has also closed.

Following the impact of the industrial revolution and railways in previous centuries, the 20th century has been affected by the motorcar and, most recently, the rise of leisure. Boston remains important as a local centre because it is so far from any larger city, the nearest being Nottingham, Peterborough and Lincoln, which are all over 30 miles away. Because of Boston's relative isolation, during the second half of the century local organisations developed a range of recreational and sporting facilities that are outstanding for a town of its size. In the beginning they were financed without help from the local council but, following the early success, further developments received financial help from the borough and county councils. All of them survive today and are largely run by volunteers. They include the Indoor Bowls Club, Boston Lawn Tennis Club, the Mayflower Sports Association, the Boston Weight Training Club and the Peter Paine Sports Hall complex, as well as Blackfriars Theatre and Arts Centre.

Towards the end of the century, the council started to exploit the tourist potential of the cultural and recreational amenities and identified part of the town as the 'Cultural Quarter'. This includes the Guildhall Museum which, since 1986, has had a curator and other staff, and in 2005 is undergoing a major refurbishment. Next to the guildhall is the magnificent Fydell House which is occupied by Pilgrim College as an adult education centre. North of the guildhall is the lively Blackfriars Arts Centre in Spayne Lane, formed in the 1960s out of the remains of the medieval Dominican friary. And across the road is the Sam Newsom Music Centre, created by Lincolnshire County Council in 1978 as the music department of Boston College to replace premises in Shodfriars Lane that were demolished for John Adams Way.

Fact File

The Sam Newsom Music Centre of Boston College is in a converted 18th-century granary that later became Lincoln's Seed Store on Packhouse Quay. It was opened in May 1978, and is named after a former director of education of Holland County Council. A memorial plaque to Sam Newsom was placed in the bar, now the reception area of the Music Centre.

In the 1990s Boston Borough Council was granted considerable funding by English Heritage under the Conservation Area Partnership Scheme and, more recently, the Townscape Heritage Initiative, and it entered

SHODFRIARS HALL c1955 B155040

into partnership with the Boston Preservation Trust and Boston Heritage Trust to ensure the preservation of a considerable number of 'buildings at risk'. This has left Boston with a substantial legacy of its historical buildings.

The fifth element of the Cultural Quarter ought to be Shodfriars Hall, a fine brick building designed by John Oldrid Scott, son of Sir G G Scott, and opened in 1874 using a restored and enlarged 16th-century half-timber building as its front of house. Arthur Lucan, who later became a stage and film star as Old Mother Riley, was born at Sibsey as Arthur Towle, and first appeared on stage at Shodfriars Hall in 1899, aged fourteen. It closed as a theatre in 1929 but is still a social club. A wider interpretation of culture might also include the Boston United football ground and the adjacent 'Gliderdrome' dance hall, where Elton John and other leading performers appeared during the second half of the 20th century.

Old Mother Riley is not Boston's only link with cinema. The town was home to Barry Spikings who produced 'The Deer Hunter' in 1978, and to Gerry O'Hara who directed 'Fanny Hill' (1983) and 'Home Alone' (1990) among others. The first films seen in Boston were shown in showmen's booths in the early 1900s, but then a number of small cinemas were built or converted from other buildings and, in the 1930s, two large ones were built, the Odeon in South Square (demolished in the 1990s) and the Regal in West Street. Film-going declined when faced with competition from television and videos,

and all of Boston's cinemas had closed at the end of the 20th century, though in 2002 the multi-screen West End cinema opened in West Street.

After Margaret Thatcher became Prime Minister in 1979, the role of local government changed. Local authorities became enablers and strategic planners of services rather than direct providers, and are selling off assets they do not need for the provision of statutory services. So Boston Dock was sold to a private consortium in January 1990, council housing was transferred to a charitable trust, and the Corporation Building (now called the Exchange Building) was sold off as well, after 200 years. The county council's old people's homes, including Ingelow Manor built in the 1960s, were transferred to the Orders of St John, a national charity formed to take them over.

Interest in promoting links between the two Bostons waxed and waned during the 20th century, and was at its greatest in the 1930s and late 1990s. During the 1930s there were a number of exchange visits between the mayors of the two Bostons and other citizens. Americans raised funds to help pay for the restoration of the Stump, and in 1931 donated the large sum of £11,000. On 22 July 1934, the Presiding Bishop of the Episcopal Church of the USA ceremonially opened the gates that still stand at the base of the tower inside the church. The gates had originally been at the entrance to the small area of pews in the centre of the church in the 18th century and, for 80 years after the 1850s restoration, they had formed the entrance to

BOSTON UNITED FOOTBALL GROUND

Boston first had a football club in the FA Cup in 1887, though it was not very successful, and by 1914 there were two teams, both based in pubs in Main Ridge, and using the ground north of that street that continued in use throughout the 20th century. The ground's name changed from 'Main Ridge' to 'Shodfriars Lane' and finally 'York Street'. In 1933 Boston F C went into liquidation, and Boston United replaced it later that year. In January 1934 Ernest Malkinson was elected to the Board, and for most of the next 70 years his family were one of the driving forces behind Boston United. After 1978, United's ground was rebuilt. The club went fully professional in 2001, and in 2002 were promoted to the Football League. In 2004 the Chairman announced plans for the club to move to a new ground next to the Princess Royal Sports Arena on the western edge of the town.

the Grammar School yard. On 18 July 1938, Ambassador Joseph Kennedy, whose son John later became President of the USA, attended the dedication of one room in Fydell House for the use of American visitors.

During the Second World War transatlantic pilgrimages were not possible, but on some occasions the American ambassador came to the Fourth of July services in the Stump that were attended by numbers of American soldiers and airmen stationed nearby, who paraded to the church. After the 1930s links between the two Bostons lapsed but, in the 1990s, new efforts were made to revive them and led to the formation of the Historic Bostons Partnership chaired by Judy Cammack, Mayor of Boston in 1995, and a similar committee across the Atlantic chaired by Professor Will Holton. There have been some exchange visits, and schools, clubs and other groups have been encouraged to contact their equivalents either directly or via the internet.

At the height of Boston's medieval prosperity many kings and queens may have visited the town without leaving us any record, but in the late 20th century much of the time of our royal family is taken up with official visits around the country. Boston has had many visits by the Princess Royal in recent years. In 1976 Princess Anne opened Pilgrim Hospital, which is one of the two largest hospitals in Lincolnshire and one of the largest employers and consumers in the Boston area. In 1995 the Princess Royal, as she now was, visited Boston to mark the 450th anniversary of the Borough's incorporation and she was back in March 2000 to open the Len Medlock Voluntary Centre, named after a local benefactor who contributed to many good causes in the town in the late 20th century. Her links with the town were finally reflected on 7 October 2003 when she opened the Princess Royal Sports Arena named in her honour. The institution of monarchy has lasted over 1,000 years, and Boston has lasted nearly as long.

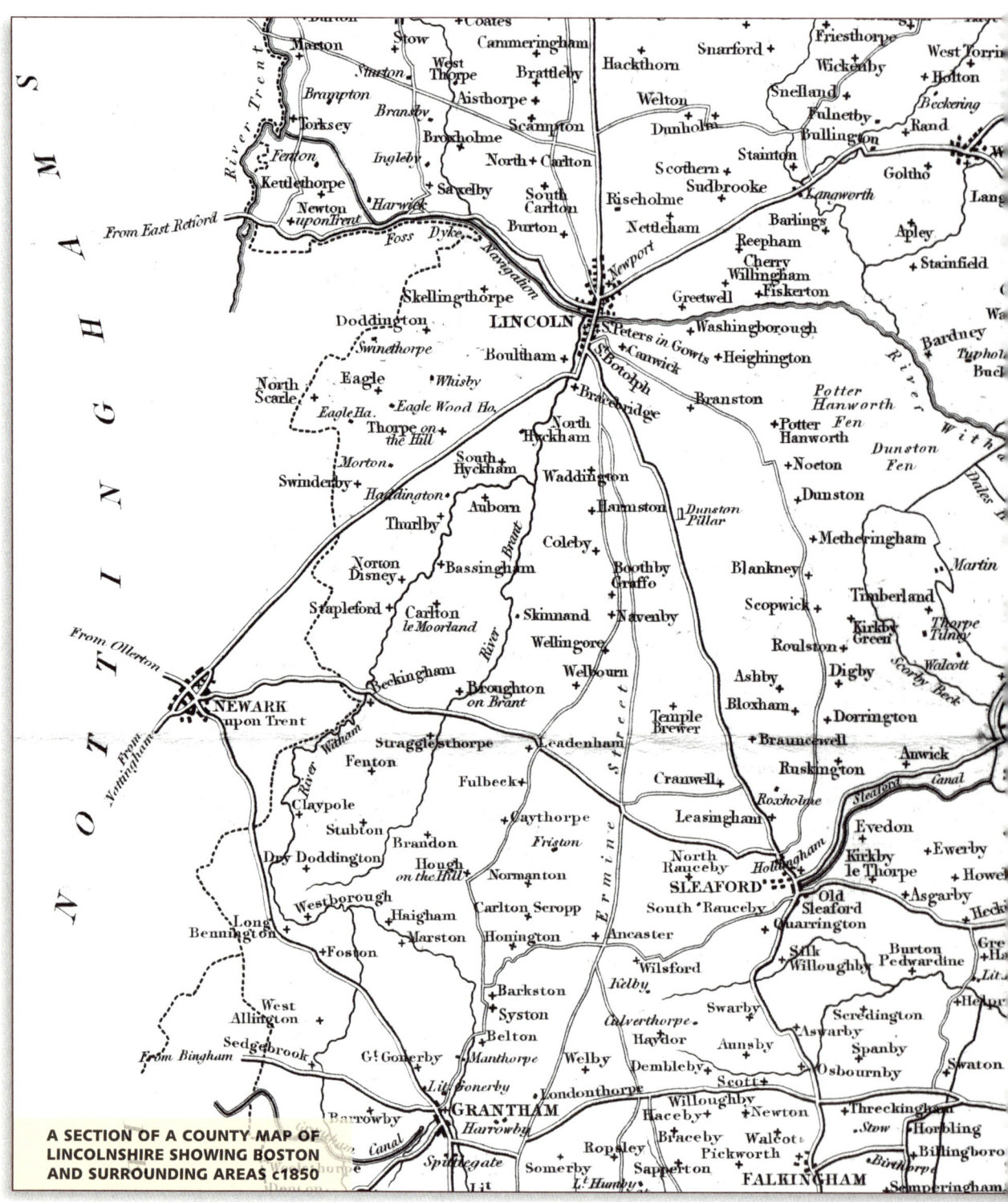

A SECTION OF A COUNTY MAP OF LINCOLNSHIRE SHOWING BOSTON AND SURROUNDING AREAS c1850

THE AUTHOR now lives away from the town, but returns several times a year and is impressed at how it is developing. Boston is returning to its historic place as a European town. Many people from Portugal and other parts of Europe have come to live and work in the area and, once again, foreign tongues are heard on its streets. This reminds us that, at several crucial periods in its history, Boston has had close links to the continental mainland. The town was created by a knight from Brittany, and the inhabitants of the area at that time were a mix of Saxons and Vikings. During its medieval heyday merchants from the Hanseatic ports of north Germany and the Baltic lived and died here, and founded some of the friaries in the town - the tomb slab of Wisselus of Smalenburg can be seen in the parish church. In the time of Elizabeth I, a group of Dutch refugees with names such as Peck and Rysdale settled in Boston, whose families stayed long in the town. During Boston's Georgian prosperity its trade was coastal, not overseas, but it attracted people who had been born in Italy and Germany as well as parts of Britain. Other ports around the coast of the United Kingdom benefited from the growth of the British Empire, but Boston's trade has always been predominantly with Europe. Since 1958 Boston has been twinned with the French town of Laval, capital of the department of Mayenne, so a European dimension is a present and future element of Boston's history.

In the late 20th and early 21st centuries, a number of industrial and business parks have been established on the edge of the town to encourage greater diversity of employment. The mechanisation of so much agricultural work has seen a rapid decline in the numbers employed in agriculture and, in recent times, there has been a great increase in 'pack-houses' where local and imported produce is processed and packaged for supermarkets. Difficulties in the recruitment of local labour has led to large numbers of immigrants being employed in the industry.

A recent brochure, produced by the Tourism and Arts Section of Boston Borough Council, tells us that Boston is rapidly cultivating a reputation as a vibrant and cosmopolitan centre for leisure by day and by night. Boston has the West End multiplex cinema as well as the Blackfriars Theatre, the Haven museum resource and arts centre and many top quality sporting facilities. For the fitness fanatic there are the Geoff Moulder Leisure Complex, that includes a superb swimming pool, a toddler pool, and a 50-yard flume slide as well as a fitness suite, and the Peter Paine Sports Centre offering activities such as squash and badminton. There is ten-pin bowling at the Boston Bowl and two 18-hole golf courses. The long and wide fenland drains near Boston have long been well-known among anglers for their bountiful supply of coarse fish. Then there is a wide range of restaurants and bars serving traditional and international cuisines, including Italian, Thai, Indian, Portuguese and Chinese.

The Lincolnshire Development Partnership has approved the spending of £780,000 of European Community money on new

CHURCH STREET c1955 B155069

facilities around South Square to attract more visitors to the Cultural Quarter. There will be distinctive signs, sculptures and visitor trails to make the most of the riverside setting, and attractive lighting will pick out features of the areas many historic buildings. In the early 21st century, the guildhall closed for a few years while a major restoration took place; this was followed by a re-arrangement of the displays, and the development of the Haven museum resource and arts centre in a building to the south of Fydell House. The borough council committed £800,000 to this project, and the

THE HISTORIC BOSTONS PARTNERSHIP

Interest in the historic links between the Bostons in Lincolnshire and Massachusetts was revived in the 19th century when local historian Pishey Thompson emigrated to the USA in 1819, and continued to research the links between the town and its daughter city. Money from old Massachusetts families contributed to the restoration of the Cotton Chapel in St Botolph's in 1857, the Guildhall Museum soon after 1900, and the tower of the Stump in the 1930s. The politicians of both Bostons visited each other's communities in the 1930s, and several new streets in the Carlton Road and Woad Farm Road areas were given names connected with both Bostons. New efforts to link the Bostons were started in the 1990s through the efforts of Professor Will Holton in Massachusetts, and John and Judy Cammack in Lincolnshire.

Heritage Lottery Fund provided just short of £1million to conserve the guildhall and improve its museum facilities. The Haven opened in the summer of 2005, and the refurbishment of the museum should be completed in late 2006.

There is also an improvement in the shopping areas. One tiny but telling detail is that most of the charity shops have left the market place, and proper shops have taken their place. The main sign of an improvement is the construction of the £22m Pescod Square shopping complex in the Mitre Lane and Silver Street area. It involved the moving of the remains of the 15th-century Pescod Hall about 100 feet to the west, and the creation of a new street in place of Silver Street. There are 23 new shops, including some national names, with a multi-storey car park above them with space for 400 cars. The first shop to open was Next women's fashions in the autumn of 2003, and the development was completed a year later, including an Ottakar's shop in Hutson's old ironmonger's premises in Wide Bargate. Pescod Hall was restored in the late 20th century by Oldrids and used for their young women's fashions, but since its move it has been occupied by Esprit, a designer ladies fashion store, and is their first store outside London.

The original plan for the Pescod Square development had included moving the GPO sorting office, but when that proved too expensive the borough council contributed the difference, up to £1.3million. This meant that Boston got a new Royal Mail sorting office off South End in place of the one that

WIDE BARGATE AND PESCOD SQUARE 2005 B155719k (Neil Wright)

The north end of the Pescod Square retail development includes the former Woolpack Inn, which became a draper's shop c1860, then Hutson's ironmongers, and is now Ottakar's bookshop.

was demolished. After 2000, a new retail area containing PC World, Aldi, Halfords, MFI, Carpet Right, Asda, eating franchises such as McDonalds, and lots of parking space was created around the railway station. Despite all these changes, the stalls of Boston's original open-air market still flourish, the largest market in Lincolnshire, as does the weekly auction on Bargate Green, illustrating the continuity between the present town and its medieval origins. It remains to be seen what impact all the new retail developments will have on locally-owned businesses.

Fact File

The statue between the parish church and the Market Place is of local-born Herbert Ingram (1811-60) who founded The Illustrated London News in 1842, the world's first illustrated newspaper. Ingram made a fortune in London but kept up his interest in Boston, and became Liberal MP for the town in 1856. The figure of a woman at the foot of his statue reflects his involvement with the Boston Water Company.

This splendid Victorian feather factory, built 1877, later became Edward Fogarty's first premises, and is now apartments.

ANDERSON'S FEATHER FACTORY, TRINITY STREET 2005 BI55720K (Neil Wright)

WATERWAYS

If current plans are carried out successfully, the old quays of the Haven could return to the important place they held for centuries in the life of the town. A new barrage will be constructed downstream, expelling the tide, and boats will be able to moor at Packhouse Quay, Doughty Quay, and other places along the Haven through the centre of Boston. The project would connect the South Forty Foot Drain to the inland waterways of the Midlands via the Welland and Nene. Boston will be on a circular waterway route from Peterborough to Lincoln, and the new barrage will allow boats to travel safely from the Black Sluice to the Grand Sluice.

Plans are also under way for economic developments that should benefit the privately owned port of Boston and the people and businesses dependent on it. During 2005 Lincolnshire Development, part of Lincolnshire County Council, prepared a bid for European funding under Objective 2 for the Boston Southern Enterprise Zone in the Marsh Lane area south of the dock. This would fund the construction of a dock link road, and the commissioning of detailed feasibility work in respect of a proposed barrage for the town. The Dock Link Road is planned to go from Spalding Road to Skirbeck Road via the dock, with a bridge over the Haven at the south end of High Street. This road will give access to the business premises along the east bank of the Haven south of the dock. The other proposal, for the construction of a barrage across the

Haven, will make it safer for shipping to moor along the dock's Riverside Quay, and also to moor at other quays through the town. The total long-term cost could be £40 million with up to £12 million to be included in the first-stage bid. The county council propose to assemble a funding package, purchase land and start building the Dock Link Road by March 2006.

Even more significant will be a proposed new road to be built round the south side of Boston, linking the Boardsides Road to the industrial area of Marsh Lane. It will include a bridge over the railway line and the South Forty Foot Drain. At present nearly all traffic to and from the Dock has to go over the Haven Bridge, and that bridge is also used by most of the traffic on John Adams Way. When the new southern road is opened, together with the 'Dock Link Road' which is really a new bridge onto the Dock, most Dock traffic will use this new road. There will be less traffic on John Adams Way which will be a great relief to the motorists of Boston. At first the new road will link Boardsides to London Road, and the extension through Calders and Grandidge's site to Spalding Road will have to wait until a later date. This new road will also enable the south-west quarter of the town near Wyberton West End Road and Chain Bridge Road to be developed to meet Boston's future housing needs.

The proposed river barrage is also necessary for the creation of an inland waterway link through the fens between Lincolnshire and Peterborough, avoiding the tidal waters of the Wash. The proposed new inland route will use the Welland, Glen and South Forty Foot Drain, plus new links from Peterborough to the Welland and from the Glen to the southern end of the South Forty Foot Drain. That will bring craft to the Black Sluice in Boston, and a barrage below that point will enable them to reach the Grand Sluice, and gain access to the Witham and connected waterways. The Haven through the town centre will no longer be totally tidal, and this will make it feasible for inland craft to moor at Doughty Quay and Packhouse Quay or at other points on the banks where facilities can be provided. This is one of several schemes by the County Council, British Waterways and other partners to greatly increase the tourist usage of the county's waterways and should benefit Boston.

It may be a few years before we see the barrage, but the Water Rail Way following the old railway line on the river bank from Lincoln to Boston, part of a national cycle route from Hull to Harwich, should be completed in 2006. The Water Rail route will include interpretation panels at points along the way, with information about history and natural history. Being elevated, the route will offer striking views of the countryside for riders and walkers, and the cycleway's smooth surface means it can be enjoyed by people with wheelchairs and pushchairs.

A positive sign for the future was the creation of the Boston Woods Trust in 2001, a long-term project to plant seven miles of native deciduous woodland, wildflower meadows and ponds in a crescent-shaped corridor to the west of the town. This will provide the people of Boston with a recreational amenity for walking, bird watching, horse riding and cycling. It is also planned to include an arboretum and country park of specimen trees dedicated to Sir Joseph Banks. The revived links with Boston, Massachusetts are also resulting in proposals to include a 'Puritan Path' of plaques in the churchyard of St Botolph's to commemorate individuals who went from here to New England in the 1630s.

For half-a-century or more Boston people have wanted a bypass for the town, and many feel that the construction of the John Adams Way inner relief road prevented them getting that in the second half of the 20th century. The need for a bypass is the biggest controversy in present-day Boston. New retail developments in the town have increased traffic congestion and people fear gridlock, but a bypass will not reduce the number coming into Boston to shop or work. If funds are now available for large scale schemes many people would prefer to see them spent on a bypass, but it is said that the external funds are only available for economic development, and could not be diverted to a bypass. The Southern Economic Corridor will enable much dock traffic to bypass the town, but the main part of the bypass is still needed from Boardsides Road north over the Witham to the Spilsby and Skegness roads. Representatives of the pressure group seeking to get a Boston bypass stood as candidates in the general and county council elections on 5 May 2005. Richard W Austin won the Boston South seat on the County Council.

THE BRIDGES

Until the 1760s the Town Bridge at Boston was the only bridge over the Witham between Lincoln and the Wash. The Town Bridge was first referred to in 1220, and has been replaced several times before the present bridge was built in 1913. The Grand Sluice, with a bridge over it, was opened in 1766; the Swing Bridge to carry the railway onto Boston Dock opened in 1884; the Haven Bridge was built in 1966; and St Botolph's footbridge in the 1970s. It is expected that the town will get its sixth bridge over the Witham in the near future as part of the Dock Link Road. There are also bridges over the various drains around the town.

Development is already taking place next to Boardsides Road on the western edge of Boston. The Endeavour Park business area was developed and opened by Broadgate Developers in October 2000; the development of this land was achieved with grants of £1.7m from East Midlands Development Agency, the European Regional Development Fund 5b programme, the Single Regeneration Budget and the borough council. The long-established local car dealers, Taylors, built attractive showrooms for their Peugeot and Citreon dealerships there, and the borough council built two linked office buildings on half of a 2.24 acre site at the entrance to the Park. The new offices, ready for letting to small businesses to move into quickly, had been built by the council in an effort to attract firms to move on to the Park.

A little to the west of Endeavour Park is the

Fact File

The dual-carriageway that was built in the 1970s and snakes its way through eastern Boston is named after the second President of the USA. John Adams was a lawyer in Boston, Massachusetts at the time of the American Revolution and a champion of liberty. His connection with Boston, Lincs, is that his wife's ancestors (named Quincy) came from this area. His eldest son John Quincy Adams became the sixth President of the USA in 1825.

Princess Royal Sports Arena, a striking £7m sports stadium. It is a world first, designed from the beginning to cater for both disabled and able-bodied athletes. The stadium will also be the new home of the town's thriving rugby club, and there will be a health and fitness centre open to the public as well as magnificent indoor training facilities. Thanks to the involvement of one of the main sponsors, Finnforest - an international company with its UK headquarters in Boston - the stadium was built from timber in Finland and shipped to the site to be assembled. The rugby club hope

their site will become a centre of excellence. In 2004, the chairman of Boston United football club announced that he also hoped to move that club to a new ground next to the Princess Royal Sports Arena.

With all this development going on, in ten to fifteen years' time Boston will have changed remarkably. The history of Boston has seen a number of booms and slumps, and now could be starting another boom. One characteristic that the author has seen over the years is that outsiders often come to Boston expecting to be here only a short time before moving on, but then find themselves entranced into staying and contributing to this distinctive self-confident and self-reliant town. Statistics show that Boston has its share of social problems and some of the most deprived areas in Lincolnshire, but it also has a lot going for it due to its very positive attitude. In about 60 years' time, Boston will have to decide when to celebrate its first 1,000 years, sometime between 2066 and 2086. What will life be like then? Will the town have got its bypass? Will the original Boston be as cosmopolitan and dynamic as its daughter city across the Atlantic? Younger readers will just have to wait and see!

TOWER STREET 1893 32065

ACKNOWLEDGEMENTS

I owe a debt to all historians who have published books on particular aspects of the history of this wonderful town, and to many other people who have helped my researches. I would particularly like to thank Ann Carlton who provided the information about Maud Foster, and John Cammack who gave me information of 20th-century developments. I am also very grateful for the support of my partner Sarah during the time I have been working on this and other projects. This book would not have been possible without the support of the History of Boston Project, the Boston Preservation Trust, and Julia Skinner of The Francis Frith Collection.

BIBLIOGRAPHY

G S Bagley, *Floreat Bostona (1985)*

G S Bagley, *Boston Its Story and People (1986)*

A M Cook, *Boston (Botolph's Town) (1948)*

A M Cook, *Lincolnshire Links with the USA (1956, 2nd ed 2005)*

D Cuppleditch, *A Century of Boston (2002)*

A A Garner, *Boston and the Great Civil War (1972)*

A A Garner, *The Fydells of Boston (1987)*

S J Gunn, *Charles Brandon, Duke of Suffolk c1484-1545 (1988)*

M Hanson & J Waterfield, *Boston Windmills (1995)*

P Meyer & J C Revell, *Boston: Its Fishermen, And The First World War (c2004)*

M Middlebrook, *Boston at War (1974)*

F Molyneux & N R Wright, *An Atlas of Boston (1974)*

W M Ormrod (editor), *The Guilds in Boston (1993)*

N Pevsner & J Harris (2nd ed revised by N Antram), *The Buildings of England: Lincolnshire (1989)*

P Thompson, *The History and Antiquities of Boston (1856, reprinted 1997)*

N R Wright, *The Book of Boston (1986)*

N R Wright, *Boston A Pictorial History (1994)*

N R Wright, *The Railways of Boston (2nd ed 1998)*

N R Wright, *Boston by Gaslight (2002)*

WEBSITES

Boston Borough Council website - www.boston.gov.uk

The Pilgrims, Official Website of Boston United Football Club - www.bufc.co.uk

Francis Frith
Pioneer Victorian Photographer

Francis Frith, founder of the world-famous photographic archive, was a complex and multi-talented man. A devout Quaker and a highly successful Victorian businessman, he was philosophical by nature and pioneering in outlook. By 1855 he had already established a wholesale grocery business in Liverpool, and sold it for the astonishing sum of £200,000, which is the equivalent today of over £15,000,000. Now in his thirties, and captivated by the new science of photography, Frith set out on a series of pioneering journeys up the Nile and to the Near East.

He was the first photographer to venture beyond the sixth cataract of the Nile. Africa was still the mysterious 'Dark Continent', and Stanley and Livingstone's historic meeting was a decade into the future. The conditions for picture taking confound belief. He laboured for hours in his wicker dark-room in the sweltering heat of the desert, while the volatile chemicals fizzed dangerously in their trays. Back in London he exhibited his photographs and was 'rapturously cheered' by members of the Royal Society. His reputation as a photographer was made overnight.

By the 1870s the railways had threaded their way across the country, and Bank Holidays and half-day Saturdays had been made obligatory by Act of Parliament. All of a sudden the working man and his family were able to enjoy days out, take holidays, and see a little more of the world.

With typical business acumen, Francis Frith foresaw that these new tourists would enjoy having souvenirs to commemorate their days out. For the next thirty years he travelled the country by train and by pony and trap, producing fine photographs of seaside resorts and beauty spots that were keenly bought by millions of Victorians. These prints were painstakingly pasted into family albums and pored over during the dark nights of winter, rekindling precious memories of summer excursions. Frith's studio was soon supplying retail shops all over the country, and by 1890 F Frith & Co had become the greatest specialist photographic publishing company in the world, with over 2,000 sales outlets, and pioneered the picture postcard.

Francis Frith had died in 1898 at his villa in Cannes, his great project still growing. By 1970 the archive he created contained over a third of a million pictures showing 7,000 British towns and villages.

Frith's legacy to us today is of immense significance and value, for the magnificent archive of evocative photographs he created provides a unique record of change in the cities, towns and villages throughout Britain over a century and more. Frith and his fellow studio photographers revisited locations many times down the years to update their views, compiling for us an enthralling and colourful pageant of British life and character.

We are fortunate that Frith was dedicated to recording the minutiae of everyday life. For it is this sheer wealth of visual data, the painstaking chronicle of changes in dress, transport, street layouts, buildings, housing and landscape that captivates us so much today, offering us a powerful link with the past and with the lives of our ancestors.

Computers have now made it possible for Frith's many thousands of images to be accessed almost instantly. The archive offers every one of us an opportunity to examine the places where we and our families have lived and worked down the years. Its images, depicting our shared past, are now bringing pleasure and enlightenment to millions around the world a century and more after his death. For further information visit: www.francisfrith.co.uk

FREE PRINT OF YOUR CHOICE

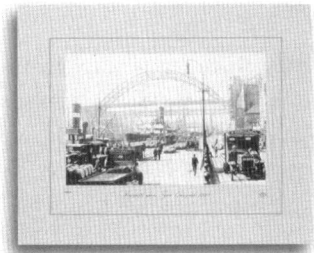

Mounted Print
Overall size 14 x 11 inches (355 x 280mm)

Choose any Frith photograph in this book. Please note: photographs with a reference number starting with a "Z" are not Frith photographs and cannot be supplied under this offer.

Simply complete the Voucher opposite and return it with your remittance for £2.25 (to cover postage and handling) and we will print the photograph of your choice in SEPIA (size 11 x 8 inches) and supply it in a cream mount with a burgundy rule line (overall size 14 x 11 inches).

Offer valid for delivery to one UK address only.

PLUS: Order additional Mounted Prints at HALF PRICE - £7.49 each (normally £14.99)
If you would like to order more Frith prints from this book, possibly as gifts for friends and family, you can buy them at half price (with no additional postage and handling costs).

PLUS: Have your Mounted Prints framed
For an extra £14.95 per print you can have your mounted print(s) framed in an elegant polished wood and gilt moulding, overall size 16 x 13 inches (no additional postage and handling required).

IMPORTANT!

These special prices are only available if you use this form to order. You must use the ORIGINAL VOUCHER on this page (no copies permitted). We can only despatch to one UK address. This offer cannot be combined with any other offer.

Send completed Voucher form to:
The Francis Frith Collection, Frith's Barn, Teffont, Salisbury, Wiltshire SP3 5QP

CHOOSE A PHOTOGRAPH FROM THIS BOOK

Voucher for FREE and Reduced Price Frith Prints

Please do not photocopy this voucher. Only the original is valid, so please fill it in, cut it out and return it to us with your order.

Picture ref no	Page no	Qty	Mounted @ £7.49	Framed + £14.95	Total Cost £
		1	Free of charge*	£	£
			£7.49	£	£
			£7.49	£	£
			£7.49	£	£
			£7.49	£	£
			£7.49	£	£

Please allow 28 days for delivery. Offer available to one UK address only

* Post & handling		£2.25
Total Order Cost		£

Title of this book . . . .

I enclose a cheque/postal order for £ . . . .
made payable to 'The Francis Frith Collection'

OR please debit my Mastercard / Visa / Maestro card, details below

Card Number

Issue No (Maestro only)   Valid from (Maestro)

Expires   Signature

Name Mr/Mrs/Ms ....

Address ....

....

....

.... Postcode ....

Daytime Tel No ....

Email ....

ISBN: 1-84589-196-1   Valid to 31/12/08

FREE PRINT - SEE OVERLEAF

CAN YOU HELP US WITH INFORMATION ABOUT ANY OF THE FRITH PHOTOGRAPHS IN THIS BOOK?

We are gradually compiling an historical record for each of the photographs in the Frith archive. It is always fascinating to find out the names of the people shown in the pictures, as well as insights into the shops, buildings and other features depicted.

If you recognize anyone in the photographs in this book, or if you have information not already included in the author's caption, do let us know. We would love to hear from you, and will try to publish it in future books or articles.

OUR PRODUCTION TEAM

Frith books are produced by a small dedicated team at offices in the converted Grade II listed 18th-century barn at Teffont near Salisbury, illustrated above. Most have worked with the Frith Collection for many years. All have in common one quality: they have a passion for the Frith Collection. The team is constantly expanding, but currently includes:

Paul Baron, Jason Buck, John Buck, Heather Crisp, David Davies, Louis du Mont, Isobel Hall, Lucy Hart, Julian Hight, Peter Horne, James Kinnear, Karen Kinnear, Tina Leary, Stuart Login, Sue Molloy, Miles Murray, Sarah Roberts, Kate Rotondetto, Dean Scource, Eliza Sackett, Terence Sackett, Sandra Sampson, Adrian Sanders, Sandra Sanger, Julia Skinner, Lewis Taylor, Shelley Tolcher, Lorraine Tuck, Miranda Tunnicliffe, David Turner and Ricky Williams.